CAMBRIDGE LIBRARY COLLECTION

Books of enduring scholarly value

Polar Exploration

This series includes accounts, by eye-witnesses and contemporaries, of early expeditions to the Arctic and the Antarctic. Huge resources were invested in such endeavours, particularly the search for the North-West Passage, which, if successful, promised enormous strategic and commercial rewards. Cartographers and scientists travelled with many of the expeditions, and their work made important contributions to earth sciences, climatology, botany and zoology. They also brought back anthropological information about the indigenous peoples of the Arctic region and the southern fringes of the American continent. The series further includes dramatic and poignant accounts of the harsh realities of working in extreme conditions and utter isolation in bygone centuries.

An Arctic Voyage to Baffin's Bay and Lancaster Sound

In 1847, Sir John Franklin and his crew perished on their Arctic expedition. The following years saw multiple attempts to discover what happened to them. First published in 1850, this short account by Robert Anstruther Goodsir (1823–95) is based on the journal he kept while serving as surgeon during an 1849 mission in search of the missing explorers. Seeking to find his brother, Harry, who was assistant surgeon and naturalist on Franklin's expedition, Goodsir vividly describes the various dangers encountered, such as ice floes, icebergs, storms and shipwrecks. Moreover, he takes note of wildlife, notably birds and fish, and records interactions with Inuit. The perspective offered by a medical man, with a keen desire to raise awareness of ongoing rescue efforts, adds further interest to the narrative. Several other works relating to the expeditions in search of Sir John Franklin have also been reissued in this series.

Cambridge University Press has long been a pioneer in the reissuing of out-of-print titles from its own backlist, producing digital reprints of books that are still sought after by scholars and students but could not be reprinted economically using traditional technology. The Cambridge Library Collection extends this activity to a wider range of books which are still of importance to researchers and professionals, either for the source material they contain, or as landmarks in the history of their academic discipline.

Drawing from the world-renowned collections in the Cambridge University Library and other partner libraries, and guided by the advice of experts in each subject area, Cambridge University Press is using state-of-the-art scanning machines in its own Printing House to capture the content of each book selected for inclusion. The files are processed to give a consistently clear, crisp image, and the books finished to the high quality standard for which the Press is recognised around the world. The latest print-on-demand technology ensures that the books will remain available indefinitely, and that orders for single or multiple copies can quickly be supplied.

The Cambridge Library Collection brings back to life books of enduring scholarly value (including out-of-copyright works originally issued by other publishers) across a wide range of disciplines in the humanities and social sciences and in science and technology.

An Arctic Voyage to Baffin's Bay and Lancaster Sound

In Search of Friends with Sir John Franklin

ROBERT ANSTRUTHER GOODSIR

CAMBRIDGE
UNIVERSITY PRESS

CAMBRIDGE
UNIVERSITY PRESS

University Printing House, Cambridge, CB2 8BS, United Kingdom

Published in the United States of America by Cambridge University Press, New York

Cambridge University Press is part of the University of Cambridge.
It furthers the University's mission by disseminating knowledge in the pursuit of
education, learning and research at the highest international levels of excellence.

www.cambridge.org
Information on this title: www.cambridge.org/9781108071659

© in this compilation Cambridge University Press 2014

This edition first published 1850
This digitally printed version 2014

ISBN 978-1-108-07165-9 Paperback

AN ARCTIC VOYAGE

TO

BAFFIN'S BAY AND LANCASTER SOUND.

Ford & George, Lithographers.

54, Hatton Garden.

VIEW OF THE DEVIL'S THUMB. —— Lat. 74°.16´. Long. 57°.56´

Drawn by W.C. Owen, M.D. from a Sketch taken on the spot. by Robert A. Goodsir.

12 Miles distant, S.E.

AN

ARCTIC VOYAGE

TO

BAFFIN'S BAY AND LANCASTER SOUND,

IN SEARCH OF

FRIENDS WITH SIR JOHN FRANKLIN.

BY

ROBERT ANSTRUTHER GOODSIR.

LATE PRESIDENT OF THE ROYAL MEDICAL SOCIETY
OF EDINBURGH.

LONDON:

JOHN VAN VOORST, PATERNOSTER ROW.

M.D.CCC.L.

LONDON:
Printed by S. & J. BENTLEY and HENRY FLEY,
Bangor House, Shoe Lane.

PREFACE.

THE following pages are extracts from a rough journal kept during the voyage, and were never intended to meet the eyes of any but those who, I well knew, would judge kindly and partially of them.

They are reluctantly and diffidently laid before the public ; but I hope that the feelings will be taken into consideration which led one brother to search for another—nay, for many brothers, for surely every one of our fellow-countrymen will welcome back *as* brothers each and all of the long missing ones.

My brother Harry having embarked with Sir John Franklin in 1845, it need not be wondered at that, as year after year wore on,

and still there came no intelligence, I, as well
as the rest of my family, began to feel anxiety.
I incidentally heard of Mr. William Penney,
master of the "Advice," of his enterprising
character and energetic disposition. I proceeded to Dundee, where I had an interview
with him, and with the managing owner of
the "Advice," Mr. Hume, to whom I am
under obligation for much kindness. I offered my services, and a few days afterwards
sailed with Mr. Penney, from whom, during
the whole voyage, I met with unremitting
kindness and attention. No one could show
more interest in the fate of our missing friends
than he did; and I have reason to believe
(from neutral parties) that he made strenuous
efforts to assist Sir John Ross and his party
in 1834. Very gratifying, then, is it to me,
and doubtless also to all who have personal
interest in the missing ships, that Mr. Penney's
energy and talent have been appreciated by
Government, and that his experience and
knowledge of the navigation of the Icy Seas,
familiar to him since boyhood, will be turned

to account in the search for the missing expedition, which he is about to conduct, and in which I am to have the pleasure of joining. Most certain am I that no exertions will be spared on his part.

I must again apologise for the meagre character of the following notes ; but I trust that my hitherto untried pen, as well as the pressure of urgent professional duties, will prove my excuse for many faults and shortcomings.

Mr. Van Voorst's kind liberality has added a Frontispiece and Map, of which I am afraid the letter-press is scarcely worthy.

Finally, my most grateful thanks are due to an old and ever kind friend, Professor Edward Forbes, for his valuable guidance of my doubtful and wavering steps through the mysteries of the " Press."

There are few indeed,—if there is even a single individual, throughout the land—who will not earnestly join me in the wish that the enterprises now on foot and so nobly supported by this country, as well as by our

generous cousin nation of the New World,
may be successful, and thoroughly successful.
Should God grant that they be so, certain it
is that many thanksgivings will be rendered
up from numerous happy homes. Mingled
bitter and sweet will be the tears shed at
meetings now well nigh despaired of. Not
a few of the old—some of the young—have
gone since the last *farewell* was said.

Much, very much, gratitude is due from
the friends and relatives of all the missing
voyagers to the noble-hearted and never-tiring
Lady Franklin, for stirring up the energies of
some, stimulating the forgetful, and shaming
the careless, into renewed efforts on behalf of
our fellow-countrymen.

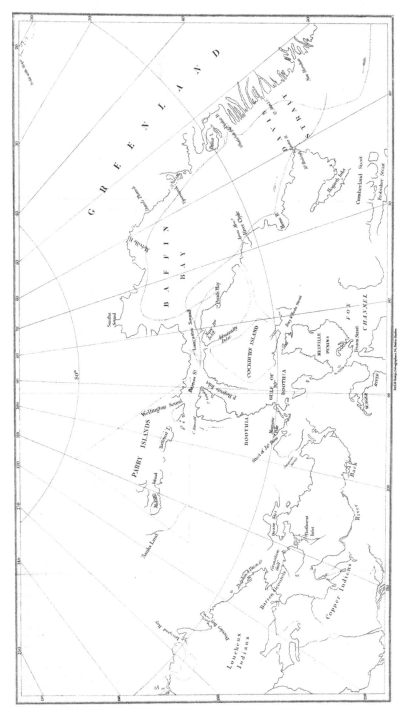

The material originally positioned here is too large for reproduction in this reissue. A PDF can be downloaded from the web address given on page iv of this book, by clicking on 'Resources Available'.

A VOYAGE,

ETC.

CHAPTER I.

WE sailed from Stromness on the 17th of March, 1849, running past Hoy Head with a light, but fair wind, and standing right to the westward. When passing the Head, or, as it is generally called, when seen from a certain point of view, the " Old Man of Hoy," I had unconsciously to perform a ceremony, usual on the occasion. One of the mates addressing me, said, " There's something on your hat," and on my taking it off to examine it, there was a general laugh ; but the captain saying, " You have now saluted the Old Man of Hoy," let me at once see what was meant.

We were soon fairly out at sea, and had a very fair run during the whole night. Next

day we could just make out the " loom "
of Cape Wrath, and the north-west part of
Sutherlandshire.

For the first ten days there was nothing
to break the daily routine of ship-life but
the changes in the weather from good to
bad, and from bad to indifferent. It was
rather tedious, as a sea-voyage always is to
a landsman, but in the good weather I could
read and write, and in the bad I managed
to make myself as comfortable as possible.

Early on the 27th of March, it came on
to blow strong, and gradually increased to a
heavy gale, so that the ship had to be " hove
to " under close-reefed main-topsail. During
the night it blew a perfect hurricane, the
wind whistling through the bare masts and
cordage with the most cutting shrillness.

On the 28th it began to moderate somewhat, but a tremendous sea was running.
About eleven o'clock I ventured on deck, and,
for the first time in my life, saw what the ocean
looks like in a storm. I could see nothing
all around but heaving mountains of water;
each succeeding wave seemed as if it would
swallow up the labouring vessel, but it always
appeared to melt away gently under us, ex-

cept when one more rapid, or " cross," would
send water and spray washing over her decks
and high up into the rigging. The motion
of the ship was not uncomfortable, being very
different from the short cross pitching we had
experienced in the North Sea. I remained on
deck about a quarter of an hour, gazing about
me in silent wonder and admiration, little
thinking that the hitherto harmless waves
were upon the very eve of proving their might
over man's puny bolts and beams. Feeling
it chilly, I went below. I had just entered
the cabin and taken my seat, when the ship
became motionless, as it were, and seemed
to tremble in every beam. A report like
thunder, mingled with the rending and crashing of timber; sudden and complete dark-
ness, with a rush of water through the sky-
light, and the ship thrown on her beam-ends,
showed me what one has to expect occasionally
at sea. I scrambled on deck after the captain,
as I best could, scarcely knowing what had
happened. Here nothing was to be seen but
wreck and destruction. The quarter-deck was
literally swept of everything, rails and bulwarks, almost all the stanchions, the binnacle,
compasses, dog's couch, and nothing could

be seen of the wheel but the nave. But
the worst was still to come, two poor fellows
were missing. One had perished unnoticed;
he must have been killed amongst the
wreck, washed overboard, and sunk like a
stone. The other had been seen by the mate,
for an instant only, floating on the binnacle, and just sinking. No human assistance
could have been rendered to them with such
a sea running. Two other poor fellows were
rather seriously injured, and took up my attention for some time. The captain, cool and
collected, soon restored confidence to his men,
and in a short time had the wreck cleared
away, a long tiller shipped, and the vessel
again hove to. Spare spars were lashed to
the stanchions that remained, so that we had
again something like bulwarks, but for many
a day afterwards the ship had a sadly damaged
and *wrecky* appearance. I have much reason
to be thankful to Providence for my escape,
for had I remained but ten seconds longer
on deck, I should either have been crushed
under the wreck, or washed overboard. Many
of the men, I dare say, were grateful enough,
but, sailor-like, in a few days all was forgotten, and "sweethearts and wives" drunk

as heartily on the Saturday nights as ever.
At any rate, we soon heard their clarionet
and songs sounding from the half-deck as
cheerily as before.

A few days after this unlucky occurrence,
we spoke a coal-laden brig, very deep in the
water, bound for some port in America, and
compared reckonings. This was quite an
event, at least to me, as it was the only vessel we had seen, and for days there had been
nothing for the eye to rest upon, except my
friends the " Mollys," of whom more anon.

Although for some time after this, we had
a succession of gales, and the ship was frequently hove to, and driven far to the southward of her course, yet I now began to feel
more at home on board, and having got my
" sea-legs" (*i. e.* able to walk the deck steadily)
was more comfortable, and could look better
about me.

I perceive in my note-book, that two days
after we left Stromness, I noticed numbers of
the Mollemoke, or fulmar petrel (*Mollemakken*,
Danish) (*Akordlak*, Esquimaux) (*Procellaria
glacialis*) following us, besides one or two passing
Rotges (*Alca alle*). When to the southward
of lat. 53°, they disappeared entirely, but when-

ever we were again to the northwards of that
parallel, the whalers' constant companion the
"Molly" again made its appearance, and we
were never without numbers of them to enliven
us, throughout the remainder of the voyage.
The fulmar of the north, except in size, may
well be likened to the albatross of the south.
Their habits and peculiarities are almost the
same. They are strong and graceful on the
wing, flying almost in the teeth of the strongest
gale, without any seeming movement of their
beautifully rounded pinions ; now swooping
along in the troughs of the sea, now skim-
ming on the snowy crests. They are almost
constantly on the wing, night and day, never
alighting on the water, except during calm
and moderate weather, and then but rarely.
They are very bold, flying close to the side of
the ship, almost within reach of the hand.
I have more than once been startled in the
evenings by one flitting close past my face,
with noiseless wing, like some gigantic moth.

At the beginning of the season, before they
are gorged with blubber, and their flesh has become rank and oily, they are occasionally killed
for food, and taste not unlike an ill-fed
chicken.

They are constantly on the look out, keeping a vigilant eye on the wake of the vessel for anything that may be thrown overboard. They are sometimes too, like the albatross, caught by a baited hook, but generally the Davis Strait's sailor has a kindly feeling for the harmless "Mollys;"* and many a reproof, strengthened generally by a not very gentle oath, have I heard the "green Orkney boys" get for molesting them during "flensing" or "making off." For it is then that they can be best seen, and their habits particularly noted. Though, previously, but a very few may be in sight, immediately upon a "fish" being struck, they begin to assemble, and are soon seen hovering over the "fast-boats" in countless flocks, and alighting to feed upon the broad pellicle of oil and blood, which forms a wake after the wounded whale. During "flensing" their boldness and impudence are often very amusing. I have seen them get on the fish, and tear at the blubber, even amongst the men's long knives, and under

* The sailors have a strange saying that the "Mollys" are animated by the spirits of "Old Greenland Skippers;" I suppose the fondness of both for blubber has led Jack to think this.

their very feet; and, more than once, I have seen one which was roughly laid hold of, and pitched out of the way with a hearty shake, coolly return again to his repast. During "making off," or the process of finally packing the blubber into the casks, when all the refuse parts or "krang" are cut off and thrown overboard, they are seen sitting in the water, in all directions, tearing at the floating pieces. They are exceedingly pugnacious, and are constantly driving one another away from any piece that may appear more tempting than another. The noise they make at such times is sometimes almost deafening, and exactly resembles that of poultry, something between the cackle of the hen and the quack of the duck, whilst the "ploutering" in the water adds to the hubbub. Hovering overhead, but never deigning to sully its snowy plumage in the greasy water, an ivory gull (*Larus eburneus*) may occasionally be seen, stooping down to a piece of "krang," which none of the fulmars may happen to be touching, pecking at it, whilst fluttering over it. The fulmars, when able to eat no more, make the best of their way to the nearest ice, where, squatted flat upon it, they sleep until ready for another gorge. The ivory gull, also, when satisfied makes its way to the ice, to rest and sleep, but takes up its position on the topmost pinnacle of the nearest hummock, when it can only be distinguished by its black legs and bill. The fulmar, graceful as it is on the wing, is the very reverse on its legs,—its walk is awkward and feeble.

We had other feathered visitors, even in the very centre of the Western Ocean, but they, poor things, were not quite so much at home there as the strong-winged fulmar. The little snow bunting (*Emberiza nivalis*) was seen fluttering about our rigging, evidently tired and exhausted, making vain efforts to alight, but always to my disappointment blown to leeward, like thistledown.

On Friday, the 13th of April, in particular, which was a fine sunny day, but very windy, with a heavy sea running, I saw no fewer than three (perhaps the same bird at different times). The third poor flutterer had almost alighted upon the lee-mizen rigging, when a violent gust blew it to leeward and astern; again it tried, and was upon the point of gaining the desired resting-place, when all at once I saw the poor little thing blown right into the sea. It rose for an instant, but its drenched feathers bore it down, and it disappeared behind the wave, as the ship forged ahead. It was so near me that I saw the glance of its eye, and it appeared to me to have an expression of suffering and exhaustion, but I dare say this was fancy on my part.

On the 14th of April we saw the first iceberg. On the afternoon of the same day we saw another of considerable size, but at some distance to windward. Being the first of these masses I had seen, I naturally regarded them with great interest. We were now approaching the most dangerous part of the voyage, "making the ice." For a week at this time, whilst rounding Cape Farewell, we had nothing but the most stormy and boisterous weather, with the additional comfort of dark nights, and the proximity of numerous huge icebergs, and what was still more dangerous, heavy "washing pieces." Both at this time and in autumn, when leaving the ice, particularly if late in the season when the nights are longer and darker, this is a most critical part of the voyage. The strictest and most vigilant look out must be kept. There are always two good hands up in the

fore-yard during the whole night to watch
for " bergs," or " washing pieces " ahead.
The latter are the most dangerous, for, as
the name implies, it is almost under water,
and the sea breaking over it; in the dark,
it is very liable to be mistaken for the broken
water on the crest of a wave. The icebergs
are exceedingly dangerous also, and many a
story have I heard of risks run, and of narrow
escapes from fatal contact with them, but
from their greater height out of the water,
and from what Dr. Scoresby calls their " natural effulgence," they are sooner and more
readily seen.

However, we got safely round the Cape,
and had a tolerable run up the Straits until
we made the ice.

CHAPTER II.

On Friday, the 20th of April, we passed
through the first "streams" of ice we had
seen. The "streams" were narrow, and the
ice of which they were composed was light.
The moment we had penetrated them we got
into smooth water, and during the whole of
the rest of the day had a beautiful run to
the northward.

The preparations for the fishing were begun
to-day by getting out the boats on to the
davits, and coiling the whale-lines, as well as
getting ready the harpoon-guns and harpoons.
There was a good deal of talking amongst
the men about the policy of commencing the
work of the season on a Friday, and not a
few of them looked rather down in the mouth.
"We shall get no fish now," says one. "Had
you ever a lucky voyage when your ship sailed

on a Friday," says another; or "hear of
any work prosper that began on a Friday."
The result, however, proved that Jack was
wrong, so that this unlucky Friday was forgotten; had it proved otherwise, coiling the
lines on Friday, the 20th of April, would have
had the whole credit of the failure. The first
operation was to get the two boats that had
been secured over the main hatchway during
the passage, hoisted out on to their davits
on the quarters. The four remaining boats
in the 'tween decks were then hoisted up,
and suspended in their respective berths on
the main-chains and waists, so that we had
three boats on each side, in addition to the
stern-boat, making seven in all. Each of
the seven harpooners having had his boat
adjudged to him by lot, with his boat's crew,
set to work to splice his lines together, and
to coil them away in the after-part of his
boat. This is done with the greatest care and
regularity, for not only are the lines valuable
and expensive originally, but when it is considered that the value of a single whale may
be from 500l. to 800l., and that if the lines
are in the slightest degree chafed or damaged,
the fish may be lost, this solicitude will not

be wondered at. Each boat's crew as they got their lines coiled, stood up and gave three hearty cheers, which were responded to by the rest of the men, so that through the day we had plenty of noise. The next operation was the "spanning" of the hand-harpoons, and the splicing on of the gun-harpoons, to the "foregangers," which are pieces of rope a few fathoms long, made of white or untanned hemp, so as to be more flexible and easily extended, when the harpoon is projected from the gun, or thrown from the hand. The harpoon-guns were then cleaned, oiled, and fastened with their swivels on the "billet heads" in the bows of the boats. Each harpooner got a supply of gunpowder and percussion-caps; and all the other requisites, which experience had taught them were necessary, were put into each boat.

The crow's-nest had, in the mean time, been got up to the main-top-gallant-mast head, and early in the afternoon we were ready, and all more than willing to attack the first unfortunate whale that should make its appearance. In the evening all the harpooners were invited down to the cabin to receive their orders and instructions for the season. Many of the harpooners are not very scrupulous when a " fish " is in question, and disputes very frequently arise between vessels on this point. This is most disagreeable to a master, who wishes to behave fairly and honourably, so that everything possible is done to prevent it. When the men had received their instructions, the steward served out a glass of grog to drink " a good voyage and a full ship." This concluded the first day of our campaign against the whales.

During the day I noticed a small bird flying about the ship, and, in spite of the bustle that was going on on deck, it alighted two or three times close to me, seemingly not at all afraid. I was thus enabled to get a good sight of it, and could make it out to be the lesser redpole (*Fringilla linaria*). It much resembles the golden-crested wren, and is almost the same size. It remained about the ship for some time, but I could not succeed in getting hold of it.

Sunday, the 22nd, was the first day we were really amongst the ice, and a very bitter day it was, blowing a gale of wind, with drifting showers of snow and sleet, and the ship under close-reefed topsails. We were tacking backwards and forwards in a deep bight amongst the ice, with scarcely any sea running, which was a comfort, indeed, after our long knocking about. The frost was intense; the ship was almost encased in ice, the bows one mass of it, and every rope electrotyped, as it were, with a silvery covering. I never, during the rest of the voyage, felt the cold so intense as on this day. Unluckily, however, the only thermometer we had on board was out of order, so that I had no means of noting the temperature.

In the evening the wind moderated, and the sea fell, when I had an excellent opportunity of observing the formation of what is called "*pancake* ice." This is admirably described by Scoresby, whose account of it I will here quote. "The first appearance of ice, when in the state of detached crystals, is called by the sailors *sludge*, and resembles snow when cast into water that is too cold to dissolve it. This smooths the ruffled surface of the sea, and produces an effect like oil in preventing breakers. These crystals soon unite, and would form a continuous sheet;

but, by the motion of the waves, they are broken into very small pieces scarcely three inches in diameter. As they strengthen many of them coalesce and form a larger mass. The undulation of the sea still continuing, these enlarged pieces strike each other on every side, whereby they become rounded, and their edges turned up, whence they obtain the name of cakes or pancakes; several of these again unite; and thereby continue to increase, forming larger flakes, until they become, perhaps, a foot in thickness, and many yards in circumference. Every large flake retains on its surface the impression of the smaller flakes of which it is composed; so that when, by the discontinuance of the swell, the whole is permitted to freeze into an extensive sheet, it sometimes assumes the appearance of a pavement.''

The 23rd was still cold, but calm and brilliantly clear. In the forenoon we crossed the Arctic Circle, and saw land for the first time (Queen Ann's Cape) since we had lost sight of Cape Wrath. We had a beautiful run during the day, through stream after stream of young bay ice, within an apparently short distance of land. Like all others inexperienced in these latitudes, I imagined we were within a short distance of the shore when we were in reality some twenty or thirty miles off.*

I had afterwards many better opportunities of noticing this phenomenon; it fully explained the stories told by Danish voyagers, of their having sailed for hours towards land, which moved from them as fast as they neared it, until, in terror, they put about, and made homewards, full of strange ideas about loadstone rocks stopping their ships and other equally improbable notions.

Here is one of the best Davis Strait cod banks, which have only recently become known, and are now resorted to by many vessels during the summer. An abundant

---

* "There is nothing more practically striking, or more captivating to the imagination, than the extreme slowness with which we learn to judge of distances, and to recognise localities on the glacier surface. Long after icy scenes have become perfectly familiar, we find that the eye is still uneducated in these respects, and that phenomena the most remarkable when pointed out, have utterly escaped attention, amidst the magnificence of the surrounding scenery; the invigoration which the bracing air produces, and the astonishing effect of interminable vastness, with which the icy plains, outspread for miles, terminated by a perspective of almost shadowless, snowy slopes, impress the mind."—PROF. JAMES FORBES.

supply of cod of the finest quality can be easily obtained, and there are in-shore excellent harbours at no great distance from the bank. Fishing here has already been found a very profitable speculation by those who have tried it; and there can be little doubt that in a short time it may prove an important branch of British enterprise.

We put our fishing-lines overboard to try for some of these cod, but it was not only too early in the season, but the ship was going too fast through the water to allow the lines to sink sufficiently, although heavily leaded. For the same reason I found that my dredge was useless, as it towed astern a short way from the surface. Whilst we were lying in Exeter harbour on the west side of Davis Strait, about the end of August, we got some of these cod from the master of the "Jane of Bo'ness." It struck me then that, although they had been some time in pickle, the mottling was much brighter than that of the cod caught in the German Ocean, and I find that my brother Harry, in his letters from Disco, of June, 1845, says that they are " mottled and speckled in the way you see the deep-sea cod at Cellardyke, *but much more strongly :* gills as red as scarlet. I never saw these organs in such perfection before, or of such a beautiful colour; few or no *Caligæ* or *Lerneæ* on them ; their stomachs full of *Hyas* and *Ammodytes.*"

The colour of the water is here of a dirty green, very different from the deep ultramarine of the ocean. As far as I can make out, it must have been somewhere in this locality that Davis found the water to be "filthy, black, and stagnating." This I cannot understand, for we certainly never saw any appearance in the water meriting this description.

Whilst passing over the Bank we saw immense flocks of ducks, principally the king duck (*Somateria spectabilis*). They were literally covering the water in myriads, but were so wild, that we could not get within shot of them. We only succeeded in killing one. I was annoyed at not being able to get a number of specimens of these beautiful birds, but did not think so much of it at the time, as my comrades told me I should get as many as I chose when we got north to the Duck Islands, where they said there were also plenty of the eider, and the long-tailed duck (*Heralda glacialis*). Eventually, however, I was disappointed; we were never near the Duck Islands, nor had I ever another opportunity of procuring skins of any of the species.

My first impressions of this country were destined to be favourable. From the time we got sight of Queen Ann's Cape, on the 23rd, until the end of the month, we had most beautiful weather. It was cold but the sunshine was bright, and the sky perfectly cloudless. The whole length of the coast we sailed along was a succession of towering mountain ranges, covered with snow, bordered by the black and precipitous shores, along which were seen the entrances to the numerous fiords deeply indenting this coast, but which, at the distance we were at, appeared to be merely valleys. The different effects of light and shade were exceedingly beautiful, more particularly in the evenings, when the summits of the more distant inland ranges shone in the sunlight like masses of gold, and the icebergs in the foreground were tinged with the most beautiful and dazzling colours. I longed for the art of the painter, and could not help fancying that Turner would have been enraptured with the magnificence of the scene.

We continued onwards to the north end of
Disco, and for nearly a month were cruising off
this island and South East Bay. Nothing can
be more delightful than sailing amongst the
ice with such weather as we had at this time.
The water is so sheltered and broken up by
the ice that, even although a smart breeze
should be blowing, it is like a mirror, and the
ship glides over it so smoothly, that you are
scarcely sensible of the rapid motion. It will
be difficult for those to conceive this who have
only seen a whale-ship lying in dock. But
even the clumsiest of these vessels looks well
when working and manœuvring in the narrow
lanes of water, amongst the ice, under a cloud
of canvas, from the royals down to the courses,
to say nothing of "flying kites," which are
bent immediately after making the ice, in order
to take advantage of the lightest breath of air.
There is always something new to be seen by
those who will look out. The water beneath
is alive with the most beautiful forms, and the
most brilliant colours. The scene around is
constantly varying, for from the immense
"floe" down to the little "sconce piece," each
succeeding one seems to assume a different
aspect; and you pass one berg of fantastic

form, only to come to another still stranger. One berg which I saw here was perforated by an arch of the most perfect outline. The berg itself was of immense size, and I am not exaggerating when I say that a pretty large vessel could pass through it, with all sails set. But it is impossible to describe the beauties of these ice islands. Many of them have caverns worn in them, within which the ice appears of the most brilliant blue and green, whilst without, all is of stainless white, the entrances curtained, as it were, with glittering icicles. The imagination of Poet or Painter never fancied grotto fitter for a Fairy Queen than these would be, could but the beauties of the Floral world be associated with them.*

All that has been said of the coral reefs of the Southern Seas may be well applied to the icy masses of the Northern; but I

* "Masses have been seen, assuming the shape of a Gothic church, with arched windows and doors, and all the rich tracery of that style, composed of what an Arabian tale would scarcely dare to relate, of crystal of the richest sapphirine blue; and often immense flat-roofed temples, like those of Luxor on the Nile, supported by round transparent columns of cerulean hue, float by the astonished spectator."—PENNANT.

much suspect it must be with the accompaniment of such weather as we at this time enjoyed, for a whistling north wind soon drives one to look for the picturesque in the neighbourhood of the cabin stove.

From this time, the 26th of April, until the middle of August, although the sun was not yet visible at midnight, we enjoyed one long continuous day. There was no part of the four and twenty hours I enjoyed more than midnight. Quietness was all around; the ship and the surrounding ice were reflected in the still water. The reflections of the few stars twinkling above seemed far beneath the smooth sea, and the scattered clouds overhead, purpled with the rays of the sun, now just dipping beneath the horizon, were so vividly pictured beneath us, that we seemed to be floating amongst them in the clear ether.

Whilst in a boat shooting seals one morning, we saw what we took to be a very large one, on a distant piece of ice. Pulling gently up to it, we were astonished that it lay so quietly, and just as I was on the point of firing, one of the men said that it was a " kajack," or Esquimaux canoe. Getting on to

the ice we found it lying upside down, as
the Esquimaux are in the habit of placing
them to keep them dry; beside it was placed
the paddle. The piece of ice was about seven
or eight yards square, and was about forty
or fifty miles from land. The canoe had been
there for some time, for the snow had gathered
up about it. Most probably the piece on
which it was lying had broken loose from
the land-ice, whilst the owner was watching
for seals, and the poor fellow would thus lose
the most valuable part of his little posses-
sions; or, as is not unfrequently the case,
he may have got adrift himself, and as the
Esquimaux from their cumbrous seal-skin
dress, are utterly unable to swim, his miserable fate may easily be conceived. We took
possession of the little canoe, and two days
afterwards, when in at the Whale Fish Islands,
we had our first visit from the natives, they
informed us that it was a Bŭnke land kajack,
recognising it from marks visible enough to
them, but not apparent to us.

The Esquimaux of these islands, and, indeed, along the whole coast, as far north
as Upernavik, are very intelligent. Many of
them can read, and some even write very

well. They are all Christians, and have a
high respect for the Danish Missionaries who
reside amongst them. I noticed in all their
canoes little slips of paper stuck into a thong,
below the round opening where they seat
themselves. Upon these there were passages
from Scripture written in Danish. Many of
them have Danish blood in them, and are
not a little proud of it. " Me half Dansk,"
" Me quarter Dansk," are common boasts
with them. The mixture, or rather the uniting
of the Scandinavian with the Esquimaux features is very curious. I noticed one man in
particular; he was taller and not so thick
set as the pure native; he had the flaxen
hair and fair complexion of the Scandinavian,
with large whiskers and beard, of which the
Esquimaux, with the exception of a thin bristling moustache, are almost destitute. But
the peculiarity of his countenance was in the
eyes; they were thoroughly Esquimaux, large,
round, and of a lustrous black. For I observed
that the eyes of the natives we saw, instead
of being small, as they are said to be in
most of the books, were large, and decidedly
the best feature in the countenance. The
other features are, however, such as they have

been described; the large head, with narrow
retreating forehead, strong coarse black hair,
flat nose, and full lips, with almost beardless
chin.

When they came along-side, a boat was
lowered in order to assist them on board.
There is a great deal of care requisite in getting out of their easily overbalanced canoes.
Two of them drawing up alongside of the
boat, the outermost inserts his paddle below
one of the thongs, which stretch across his
neighbour's deck, thus steadying the canoe
until its occupant has cautiously got out of it.
The next comer is assisted in the same way,
and the last of the party, by the aid of a companion, leaning over the gunwale of the boat,
and holding the kajack until he extricates himself from his apparently cramped position.
They always render one another this assistance
in the kindliest manner possible, but of course,
when by themselves, as they must often necessarily be, they must steady themselves
against the ice the best way they can. Their
canoes were then handed on deck, when each
owner produced from the recesses of his bark
what he had with him as barter, or, as the
sailors call it, " troak;" consisting of seal-

skins, seal-skin trowsers, caps, slippers, gloves, and tobacco-bags or "doises." These last and the slippers seemed to be in greatest demand. All these articles are made of seal-skin, and are very neatly sewed with the sinew-thread. The slippers are made of white, red, and blue leather, prepared in Denmark, and are very prettily embroidered and trimmed with fur. The men bartered for them gaudy yellow, and red pocket-handkerchiefs, old clothes, biscuits, coffee, and earthenware bowls. I had brought with me some cheap clasp-knives and sailmakers' large needles, thinking that they would be the most acceptable to the skin-sewing Esquimaux, but like many another speculator, I found that I had not known my market, as they looked with contempt at my big needles, and would scarcely have them in a present. Small sewing needles, however, were much in request, as also were cotton handkerchiefs of the most glaring colours, which most of the men had provided for this purpose.

From their frequent intercourse with the whale-ships, most of the natives here can make themselves understood, and the sailors knowing a few words of Esquimaux, they manage between them to be intelligible to one another. They informed us that the winter had been a severe one, and also that they had been somewhat short of provisions, as the Danish governors of the different colonies, fearing that the unsettled state of affairs in Denmark might prevent the vessels coming out with their annual supplies, had not given them their usual allowances of bread, &c. All the Danes here were naturally very anxious for European news, and almost all the natives whom we saw had letters or verbal messages for us, requesting intelligence whether their " beloved native country was still implicated in war." We explained the state of matters in the best way we could, to the most intelligent of our visitors, and sent one or two of the newspapers we had on board, which contained the latest Danish intelligence, to the nearest missionary, Mr. Norsted, at Bunke Island.

One would think that the inclement rigour of this country could not be very favourable to missionary enterprise, yet from the 3rd of July, 1721, when the " Arctic Apostle," Hans Egede, landed in Baals River, there have never been wanting men willing to devote

themselves to the conversion of the Esquimaux, and they have succeeded in spread-
ing Christianity as far north as the seventy-
fourth degree of latitude.

> " Fired with a zeal peculiar, they defy
> The rage and rigour of a polar sky,
> And plant successfully sweet Sharon's rose,
> On icy plains, and in eternal snows."
>   COWPER.

In how different a place is the lot of
these men cast from that enjoyed by our
own missionaries in the sunny islands of the
Pacific!

The month of May was ushered in by the
most inclement weather, — snow and biting
cold north winds, which, with the exception of
an occasional good day, continued throughout
the month. On May-day morning the sailors
had a sort of saturnalia, which they annually
enjoy at this season on board the whale-ships.
For some days previous they had been preparing an immense garland of party-coloured
ribbons fastened on a hoop, which was surmounted by a full-rigged little ship fixed on
a pivot. As twelve o'clock struck this was
suspended to the mizzen-stay, and immediately afterwards a bellowing sound was heard

ahead, and the ship was hailed. On being duly answered, Neptune and Amphitrite, or Mrs. Neptune, as they unceremoniously call her, came on board over the bows; the former a huge, red whiskered cooper's-mate, dressed in anything but classical costume, with an enormous speaking-trumpet in one hand and the trident in the other, surmounted—by a red herring. Mrs. Neptune was personated by the boatswain, with a cockernony of paper on his head, and his chin bound round with a bandage, which was stuck full of sharp iron spikes, it being her privilege to claim a kiss from each of the uninitiated after they have been duly shaved by Neptune's valet. Having previously got the captain's permission, they then proceeded to assemble all the newcomers in the 'tween deck, where they were confined in the cable tier, and one by one taken out to undergo the rough treatment of the barber, whose plentiful lathering of tar and notched iron hoop were anything but gently applied. However, it was all done in good humour, and we heard of no quarrelling amongst them, although they were certainly noisy enough during the best part of the night.

On the 6th of May we landed at Leifly, the principal Danish settlement, and the residence of the Inspector of the Colonies. I had on this occasion an excellent opportunity of marking the deceptive appearance of the land and the difficulty of judging of its distance. From the ship we appeared to be almost under the overhanging precipices, and close to the shore. Nevertheless, it was nearly an hour and a half, hard pulling, with a willing crew, and a swift boat, ere we got to the landing place.

We passed many large and beautiful icebergs aground. I was informed that in South-East Bay, in the entrance to Waygate Strait, there are large glaciers, which, if correct, would account for the number and size of the bergs generally found in this bay. It was in South-East, or, as it is generally called, Disco Bay, that the two immense bergs mentioned by Crantz remained stationary for a number of years aground in 300 fathoms water; one of which was called by the sailors Haarlem and the other Amsterdam.

We landed in a small creek, beside a number of Esquimaux huts, and a little to the southward of the flag-staff on Leifly Point.

On our landing a gentleman came up and
addressed us, whom we afterwards found to be
Dr. Rink, of Copenhagen, who had been here
for two seasons, and intended to remain
another. He was working at the Mineralogy
of West Greenland. He had spent some
years in India, and spoke English fluently.
Of course his first question, after the usual
greeting, was about the Danish and Schleswig-
Holstein war. We gave him what information
we could, whilst walking across to Leifly to
the inspector's house.

A number of Esquimaux women were standing on the rocks when we landed. Some of
the oldest of them were certainly the most
hideous-looking creatures I ever saw, although
one or two half-caste girls amongst them were
almost comely. They were dressed in seal-
skins like the men, and had their hair gathered
into an immense top-knot. Their huts were
as good, indeed better, than many I have seen
in the West Highlands of Scotland. I regret
now that I did not manage to get a view of
their interiors, but I must confess that the ac-
cumulation of filth around them deterred me.
Most of the huts were almost half built of the
bones of the whale, and whole troops of half-

starved and wolfish-looking dogs were prowling about.

We were met by the Inspector and the Governor, a short distance from their houses, and were very kindly welcomed by them. We spent some hours very pleasantly with the former and his family, consisting of his wife, her sister, and a little daughter. The Inspector himself spoke English well, so that we had no difficulty in making ourselves understood, and we were soon seated at table in the midst of a family circle, such as I little expected to have fallen in with here, refined, hospitable, and good-hearted. We were waited on by a little half-caste servant girl, neatly dressed in seal-skin trowsers, and ornamented boots, with a coloured cotton jacket, and her hair dressed in the usual top-knot. She had been the previous season in Denmark, and they gave us an amusing account of her description of the grandeur and magnitude of Copenhagen on her return. Of course we had plenty of news to tell them, in the stirring events of the previous autumn and winter, and the few newspapers we had to spare were more than acceptable. We bade them farewell, highly gratified with our visit, the only unpleasant effect of which

was, that "roughing it" on board ship was
not, for a time, so agreeable after the glimpse
of home comforts we had seen.

Everything was as yet covered with snow.
Spring had not made the slightest advances,
but I could easily conceive that this must be a
very interesting spot during their short summer. The Inspector's house faces the harbour,
which is completely land-locked, and has the
appearance of an inland loch. On the opposite
shore rises abruptly the highest range of
mountains in the island. In walking over to
the boats again, the only plant of any kind
that I could see, was the ground willow (*Salix
arctica*) peeping in some places out of the
snow; but I was informed that in the Inspector's and Governor's gardens, they grow
large cabbages, turnips, carrots, and parsnips,
besides various salads.

The bare part of the rocks we passed over
was all polished, and showed evident marks of
the action of ice. There were scattered about
many very large travelled blocks of red granite,
which was besides the only formation we saw
anywhere. The rocks along the shore also,
are in many places scratched and polished for
some feet above the level of the sea.

Whilst in South-East Bay we saw great
numbers of the white whales (*Delphinapterus
beluga*).   They are gregarious, being seldom
seen singly, but in "runs" of three or four.
They are of a dirty white, or yellowish colour,
and swim very rapidly, remaining but an instant at the surface to blow, rising three or
four times in quick succession.   I fired frequently at them, but they are exceedingly
difficult to hit from the deck; it is easier from
the crow's-nest, or the top, as you see them
in the act of rising through the clear water.
When looking down upon them in this way,
their motions can be seen to be exceedingly
graceful, and involuntarily put one in mind of
the fabled mermaid.   We saw a few narwhales
also (*Monodon monocerus*), and most of the
other ships had killed a few walruses when
passing Reef Kholl, but we unluckily did not
get a single specimen of either.

After this we ran north, as far as Hare
Island, in North-East Bay, but were stopped
by the ice, when we had to put about and
make to the southward, which, however, we
had no cause to regret, as it was the means
of our getting two large whales.   We were
more successful a second time in getting

through the barrier of ice, and into the Black
Hook (Swartzhoak) water, where we also got
" two fish at a fall." However, I will defer
saying anything of the admirable and exciting
sport of whale hunting, until we get to Ponds
Bay, into the thick of them.

The mate, during the voyage out, had told
me of a strange occurrence that had happened
here. He said that, when lying with his
ship in North-East Bay, in 1834, about six
or seven miles from the shore, along with a
number of other vessels, they were startled
by a distant rumbling noise like thunder,
which lasted a considerable time ; that shortly
afterwards a number of rolling seas came
tumbling out from the shore, and the water
around became stained, like that at the mouth
of a river after a flood. There can be little
doubt, I think, that this must have been a
débacle, equal perhaps in violence and extent
to that of the Dranse in Switzerland, in 1818,
but happening, luckily, in a country where
there were none to suffer from its effects. It
would have been interesting to have landed
here, traces of its effects might still have
been seen ; but, unfortunately, it was not
in my power.

For some time back, as I have mentioned before, there had been little difference between night and day, but it was not until the 10th of May, that we saw the

> " ——— Midnight, Arctic sun
> Set into sunrise." *

---

* Tennyson's *Princess.*

CHAPTER III.

" The men were saved. The other ships were in great
danger. The seas, mustering armies of ycie souldiers to
oppresse them, using other naturall stratagemes of fogges
and snowes to further these cruell designes."

PURCHASE'S *Pilgrims.* SIR MARTIN FROBISHER'S
Voyage in 1578.

ABOUT the beginning of June we left the
Black Hook fishing-ground, to endeavour to
effect a north passage to the west side of
Baffin's Bay. We passed Women's Islands
and Upernavik (the most northern Danish
settlement) during thick weather, and, much
to my disappointment, we had not an opportunity of landing at either of these places.
I was anxious to examine the Runic monument on Kingiktorsoak, one of the Women's
Islands, as well as the ruins at Upernavik
mentioned by Humboldt in his " Cosmos,"
and which would seem to prove, that the
discoveries of Baffin, of Ross, and of Parry,

had been anticipated by the Northmen by many centuries.*

It may be as well to explain here why it is that this north route is taken. On looking at the map it will very naturally suggest itself to one, that a much more expeditious and shorter passage to Ponds' Bay, and the coast to the southward, which it was now our object

---

* The activity, courage, and enterprising spirit of the adventurers from Iceland and Greenland is manifested by the fact, that after they had settled so far south as 41° 30″ N. latitude, they prosecuted their researches to the latitude of 70° 55′ on the east coast of Baffin's Bay, where, on one of the Women's Islands, north-west of the present most northern Danish settlement of Upernavik, they set up three stone pillars, marking the limits of their discoveries.   The Runic inscription on the stone discovered there in the autumn of 1824, contains, according to Rask, and Fin Magnusen, the date 1135.   From this eastern coast of Baffin's Bay the colonists very regularly visited Lancaster Sound, and a part of Barrow's Straits, for purposes of fishing more than six centuries before the adventurous voyage of Parry.   The locality of the fishery is very distinctly described, and priests from Greenland, from the bishopric of Gardar, conducted the first voyage of discovery.   This most north-western summer station is called Kroksfiardar-Heide.   Mention is made of the driftwood (doubtless from Siberia), which was collected there, and of the abundance of whales, seals, walruses, and sea-bears (page 234); also note, 367, of Humboldt's " Cosmos," vol. ii. Sabine's edition.

to reach as soon as possible, would be by
pushing northwards, along the west side of
Davis' Strait, and Baffin's Bay. But it has
been found from experience that it is impossible to take that course in consequence
of the immense fields of drifting ice, which
occupy the centre of Baffin's Bay, and go by
the name of the "middle ice;" being in the
early part of the season packed close to the
west shores, in consequence of the then prevailing winds. It has been found easier then,
although it is much more circuitous, to proceed up the east side, between this "middle
ice" and the land ice, or that ledge of ice
which remains during the greater part of
the season attached to the shores in varying
breadths.

On the 8th of June, we were in lat. 74°,
off the Devil's Thumb.* This extraordinary
landmark is a column of rock rising abruptly
from amongst the mountains, at a short distance from the shore, and towering above
them to an immense height. It somewhat resembles in shape one of the Standing Stones
of Stennis, or the similar Standing Stones of
Lundin in Fifeshire. We passed it on a

* Frontispiece.

beautifully clear morning, about ten or fifteen
miles off. I am not aware that any one has
landed here, at least, I can find no mention
of it in any of the earlier or later voyages,
except in one instance, where it is spoken
of as a rocky promontory. I took a rough
sketch of it from the crow's-nest, which will
give some idea of this strange feature of a
coast, wild and strange enough otherwise.
We were now fairly embarked in the passage
through Melville Bay, a part of the voyage
which is viewed by the whalers with the
greatest dread. This will not be wondered
at when it is considered that since 1819, when
it became customary for the vessels employed
in this trade to push thus far north, not a
year has passed without being marked by
more or less damage sustained by the ship-
ping between the 74° and 76° of lat. Should
a south-west or southerly wind set in whilst
they are slowly working their way through,
between the land-ice and the loose floes, it
frequently drives in the middle ice upon them,
with such violence and rapidity, that the
vessels are crushed between them like egg-
shells. In 1819, fourteen ships were thus
entirely lost; in 1821, eleven; in 1822, seven;

but the year 1830 was peculiarly disastrous. In that year nineteen vessels were entirely lost, and twelve seriously damaged; the value of the former, and the cost of the repairs of the latter, amounting to 142,600*l*. The account of these losses, given in the Edinburgh Cabinet Library, is substantially a correct one, and agrees with what I have heard from many of those, who lost their ships on that occasion.

" On the 19th June a fresh gale sprang up from the S.S.W. and drove in upon them masses of ice, by which they were soon beset, in lat. 75° 10″ N., long. 60° 30′ W., about forty miles to the southward of Cape York. They ranged themselves under the shelter of a large and rugged floe, having water barely sufficient to float them. Here they formed a majestic line behind each other, standing stem to stern so close as to afford a continued line along the whole of their decks, being at the same time so pressed against the ice that in some places a boat-hook could with difficulty be inserted in the interval.

" On the evening of the 24th the sky darkened, the gale increased, the floes began to overlap each other and press upon the ships

in an alarming manner. The sailors then
attempted to saw the ice into a sort of dock,
where they hoped to be relieved from the
severe pressure; but soon a huge floe was
driven upon them with a violence completely
irresistible. The 'Eliza Swan' received the
first shock, and was saved only by the floe
raising her completely up. It caused her,
indeed, to strike with such force against the
bow of the 'St. Andrew' that her mizzen
mast was nearly carried off, but it then passed
from under her, after damaging severely her
stern and keel. It next struck the 'St.
Andrew' midship, breaking about twenty of
her timbers and staving a number of her
casks, but it then fortunately moved along
her side and went off by the stern. Now,
however, pursuing its career, it reached successively the 'Baffin,' the 'Achilles,' the
'Ville de Dieppe,' and the 'Rattler,' and
dashed against them with such tremendous
fury that these four noble vessels, completely
equipped and fortified, and which had braved
for years the tempests of the Polar deep, were
in a quarter of an hour converted into shattered fragments. The scene was awful, the
grinding noise of the ice tearing open their

sides, the masts breaking off and falling in
every direction, amid the cries of 200 sailors,
leaping upon the frozen surface, with only
such portions of their wardrobe as they could
snatch in a single instant. The ' Rattler ' is
said to have become the most complete wreck
almost ever known. She was literally turned
inside out, and her stem and stern carried to
the distance of a gunshot from each other.
The ' Achilles ' had her sides nearly pressed
together, her stern thrust out, her decks and
beams broken into innumerable pieces. The
' Ville de Dieppe,' a very beautiful vessel,
though partly filled with water, stood upright
for a fortnight, and the greater part of her
provisions and stores were preserved, as were
also some of those of the ' Baffin,' two of
whose boats were squeezed to pieces. All
the other boats were dragged out upon the
ice, and were claimed by the sailors as their
only home. Not far from the same spot
the ' Progress,' of Hull, was crushed to
atoms by an iceberg.

" On the 2nd of June, and on the 18th of
the same month, the 'Œenhope,' also of that
port, became a total wreck. About the same
time, and within a short distance of the above,

eleven other vessels were destroyed under circumstances precisely similar.   Yet it is a
remarkable and gratifying fact, that in the
whole of these sudden and dreadful disasters
there should not have occurred the loss of a
single life.   The very element, indeed, which
destroyed the vessels was in so far propitious
as it afforded to the crews a secure, though
uncomfortable retreat.   By leaping out upon
the ice in the moment of wreck, they all
effected their escape.   Still, we have heard
of several instances in which the danger was
close and imminent.   Sometimes the seamen,
before they could snatch their clothes and
bedding, found themselves up to their middle
in water.   The surgeon of the ' North Britain'
beheld the ice rushing in and meeting from
opposite quarters in the cabin before he was
able to make his retreat."

The shipwrecked mariners, nearly a thou-
sand in number, were now obliged to establish
temporary abodes on the surface of that rough
and frozen sea, where their ships had been
wrecked.   They erected tents of sails detached
from the broken masts; they kindled fires,
and procured provisions, either out of their
own shattered vessels, or from those of their

companions, which had fortunately escaped.
But still their situation, though not desperate,
was dreary in the extreme, like outcasts in
the most desolate extremity of the earth, without any assured means, either of subsistence
or return. Yet such is the elastic spirit of
British tars, that as soon as the first shock
was over, they began with one consent, to
enjoy themselves, exulting in the idea of
being their own masters. Finding access, unfortunately, to considerable stores of wine and
spirits, they commenced a course of too liberal
indulgence. The rugged surface of the Arctic
deep was transformed into a gay scene of fes-
tivity. The clusters of tents with which it
was covered, the various scenes of ludicrous
frolic, the joyous shoutings of the British
sailors, and the dances and songs of the French
suggested the idea of a large fair; some even
gave it the name of Baffin Fair. The French-
men are said to have declared that they had
never been so happy in their whole lives. Ex-
cursions of considerable extent were made over
the ice from one party to another; a communication was even opened between the
northern and southern detachments of the
fleet, and so regularly carried on, as to be

called by the latter the "North Mail." Such
are the casualties to which the whale-ships are
yearly exposed, it may be easily conceived,
therefore, that it is with no very comfortable
feelings that they look forward to the passage
through "the Bay," as they call it. It must
necessarily, too, be a period of great anxiety
for the masters, for not only does the success
of their voyage depend upon their energy and
activity here, but the absolute safety of their
ship, upon their constant watchfulness. It
follows, therefore, that he who is the best
navigator amongst ice must necessarily be the
most successful whale-fisher.

An ominous preparation was made about
this time; sundry casks of provisions, preserved meats, bread, &c., were hoisted on
deck, and secured there, ready to be rolled
on the ice, should the *nip* come. Experience
has taught them that it is better to be thus
prepared than to trust the precarious chance
of picking them up from the hold after the
crash has taken place. I got a hint, too,
to have a bag of clothes "handy" to pitch
on to the ice.

There were eleven "sail" in company with
us, and it was an animated scene to see them

all crowding sail and threading their way out
and in amongst the floes. We continued in
company for about a week, when four of the
vessels taking a different "lead" separated
from the rest of the fleet. It came on thick
and stormy weather afterwards, when we had
all to get into docks. It was reported amongst
the ships in our company, that two of the
four vessels astern had been seen with heavy
"lists," during a temporary blink of clear
weather, and that their boats and the men's
chests had been seen lying on the ice around
them, which rendered it but too likely that
they had been caught in a "*nip.*"

This proved but too true, for, nearly two
months afterwards, when one of them rejoined
us in Pond's Bay, we heard that they had
all four been subjected to a heavy pressure, two
of them utterly destroyed, and the other seriously damaged. Our informant's vessel being
only kept afloat by two additional pumps,
taken out of one of the wrecks, and thrumbed
sails under her bottom. Had they taken the
"lead" the rest did, they would have escaped,
—had we followed them, there might have
been seven or eight vessels lost instead of
two, and even had we escaped, we might

D

have been detained so long, that ere we got
to Pond's Bay, it would have been too late
for a successful fishing: for it has been
noticed that there is little chance of getting
whales there, unless the ships arrive before
the middle of July. It may be seen by this,
how much depends upon a master being
able to pick out the best "lead," or, in
other words, to take the shortest and least
dangerous way amongst the ever-shifting floes.
But he must, besides, be able to calculate
what their probable motions will be for some
time to come, judging from the prevailing
current or wind, and marking whether they
are rotating upon themselves, or moving di-
rectly one way or the other.

Pushing our way slowly northward, we now
began to see immense fields of ice, of a dead
unbroken level, often as far as the eye could
reach, sometimes sparkling with a bright and
blinding glare in the sun, but as often lying
outstretched beneath rolling volumes of thick
mist. We would be now progressing rapidly
under a press of sail in almost open water, in
a short time afterwards closely beset by ice,
without a pool within sight for miles around.
The rapidity with which the scene thus some-

times changed, was sometimes very extraordinary. To an inexperienced eye, there would be no appearance of an immediate stoppage, but soon the water about us could be seen to be rapidly narrowing, and frequently we were scarcely secure in a dock ere the concussion would take place, and the floes were grinding and crushing against one another with the most irresistible force. It was a strange feeling to stand beside the place where such forces were in operation. It seemed like a trial of strength between the opposing floes, the hollow grinding noise under one's feet booming lower and lower in the distance. It was as if one was standing over the site of an earthquake. The ponderous ice, trembling and slowly rising, would rend and rift with a sullen roar, and huge masses, hundreds of tons in weight, would be heaved up, one above the other, until, where it was before a level, an immense rampart of angular blocks became piled.

> " And, hark ! the lengthening roar continuous runs
> Athwart the rifted deep : at once it bursts,
> And piles a thousand mountains to the clouds."

One might almost think that the poet of

the " Seasons " had witnessed such a scene.
Great misshapen columns, like those of Stone-
henge, are not unfrequently seen reared on
end, on the top of these ramparts, poised
so delicately, that a slight touch will send
them thundering down on either side. When
the pressure is lessening and " taking off,"
the hollow grinding noise becomes sharper
and shriller, and the smaller fragments are
seen slipping down between the larger; then
the topmost heavy blocks are, one by one,
launched into the chasm, which slowly widens,
and opens up, showing a long lane of water,
edged on each side by a wall of ice, formed
of the pieces which have been upheaved on
to the floe during the pressure. The spot
where this is taking place, is naturally one
of interest to the crews of the ice-bound ships,
and parties may always be seen going and
returning from the "nip" where the first
appearance of "taking off" is anxiously looked
for, as then they will be able to push forwards
to the wished-for " north water."

Cutting a dock is generally a time of hurry
and excitement, for it is not always certain
whether they be able to get the ship secured
ere the moment of danger arrives ; and besides,

as there are generally three or four vessels together, and each of their crews are shouting some strange sea ditty, to the grating and rattling of their saws, it forms a scene of strange bustle and confusion. When it becomes necessary to form a dock, all hands are immediately called; the master and the carpenter get on to the ice, and measure out its length and breadth. The triangles or tripods, and the ice saws are in the mean time handed on to the ice, the former about twelve feet high, and the latter about fourteen feet long, and six inches broad, and about a quarter of an inch thick, with two cross handles inserted into sockets at the top. The triangles are erected at the edge of the ice, and the saws suspended from them by an iron chain and pulley. To the other end of the chain are fastened a number of short ropes, each of which a man lays hold of; four or five lay hold of the cross handles, and they immediately commence work, the men with the ropes elevating the saw, the others shoving it downwards. One of them immediately strikes up a song, in the chorus of which the rest join, and it is astonishing how rapidly a well-drilled ship's company will cut through floes, from six

to eight feet thick. As they advance, the triangles are from time to time moved backwards
from the edge of the floe, until they have sawn
out the whole length of the dock, when they
saw it across at the end, and drag or push the
separated piece out. But it may happen that
there is not sufficient open water to allow
them to drag out the piece past the ship entire,
so that they have to saw it up into segments,
and draw them out of the way separately.
The ship is then towed in stern foremost; and
should there be any appearance of a very
heavy pressure coming on, the ice at the head
of the dock under the stern is sawn into dia-
mond-shaped pieces, which enables the vessel
to sustain the shock with greater ease, as she
either rises over them, or displaces them on to
the floe. Whenever this becomes at all likely
to happen, or indeed whenever a ship becomes
"beset," the rudder is unshipped, and slung
across the stern, as it is almost certain to be
the first thing damaged under these circumstances. In order to facilitate this operation,
the rudder-case of a whaler is made large and
roomy, and with the assistance of the capstan
and windlass they speedily remove it out of the
way of injury.

During the whole of the month of June
were we thus tediously working our way
through this tiresome barrier of ice, now lying
for days together fast bound in a dock, now
advancing perhaps for a few miles, by dint of
laboriously heaving with windlass and capstans
on warps and ice-claws taken out ahead.
Some days we could get on briskly enough,
alternately tracking and towing, according to
the state of the ice ; the former being done by
all the men on the floe, dragging the ship
forwards by a rope attached to the foremast,
and the latter by all the boats towing ahead.
Every slack of the ice was taken advantage of,
and no opportunity was lost of getting forwards for however short a distance.   I thought
it was desperately hard work for the men, but
was informed that it was trifling to what it is
some years when they have to track and tow
often for days and nights together, frequently
dragging their ship after them in this way for
five or six hundred miles, and that when sinking over the instep into the snow, which covers
the rugged surface of the floe.

During our frequent stoppages, if there happened to be a pool of water near, we were sure
of getting plenty of the little auk *(Alca alle)*,

which was often found literally blackening the
water, and their sharp shrill cry sounding
through the mist, when they appear to be
much more vociferous, often led us to these
pools. More than once, whilst we were " beset " where there was some extent of water,
I have in the course of an hour or two killed
four or five hundred of these birds. They fly
generally in flocks, their flight being sharp and
rapid, and never at any great distance from
the surface of the sea. In the water, they are
exceedingly active, ducking and jerking about
with a strange and rapid motion. In diving
they use both wings and feet, and cleave their
way under the water with the utmost velocity.
I found eggs fully developed in almost all the
females. They do not seem to rest during the
night, for they were then as numerous in the
pools as during the day, and incessantly flying
backwards and forwards from the distant cliffs,
which form their breeding-places. To my
great regret, I was not able to visit any of
these breeding-places, so that I did not succeed in getting specimens of the eggs of any
of the Arctic birds. The loom *(Uria troile)*
was shot occasionally, but it was not nearly
so numerous as the Rotge. The doveca,

also (*Uria grylle*), seems to become less numerous as we advance northwards. But we still occasionally see the fulmar petrel and snow-bird. The rotge and loom are shot in immense numbers by the whalers, with whom they are a favourite dish, and form an agreeable change of diet. When they have been kept some time, and are parboiled before being broiled, they eat very well, and with but little fishy flavour. I only trust that they were as plentiful with Sir John Franklin's ships as they happened to be with us at this time, when every ship in the fleet had their "davits" strung with hundreds of them.

On the 1st of July we came in sight of Cape York, lat. 75° 55′, the first land we had seen since losing sight of the Devil's Thumb. An immense number of stupendous icebergs were aground off the Cape. Two natives came on board here of the Ross tribe of Arctic highlanders, I suppose; one a stout, comely young fellow of twenty, and the other a curious-looking little man of about forty, very lame from the effects of a fall from a cliff. They seemed to differ slightly in any respect from the Esquimaux of the southern tribes; unluckily, however, I saw but little of

them, as I happened to be called away at the
time to see some men belonging to one of the
other vessels who had met with an accident.
Some of the boats belonging to the few vessels
who escaped the disasters of 1830, and succeeded in getting thus far, happened to land
to the northwards of Cape York. A short
distance from the shore they perceived some
Esquimaux huts. Advancing, they were rather
astonished at the unusual stillness which
reigned around them, they missed the usual
vociferous greetings of the natives, as well
as the noisy howlings of the half-fed dogs.
The very snow before the entrances of the
miserable skin huts was untrodden and un-
stained. They were surprised at this, but
were still more so, when, on entering the
huts, they found their inmates stark and stiff.
At first they thought them to be asleep, but
the sunken eyeballs, and the uncovered lip-
less teeth, proved that even the cold of this
desolate region could not for ever arrest the
finger of decay. Hut after hut, of the three
or four, presented the same spectacle, each
containing four or five lifeless bodies, old and
young, all evidently long dead. What had
caused this mortality could not be learned,

it had not been from starvation, for their usual food was lying about in abundance. Neither could it be ascertained whether any had escaped the strange fate of their companions, it seemed but too probable that the last survivor, after seeing friend and relative drop around him, must have himself lain down to perish alone and unassisted. It must have been a strange scene. Even the rough Greenland sailor, when telling me, nineteen years after, spoke gently and quietly of it.

By the 3rd we had rounded Cape York, and were sailing past the " Crimson Cliffs " of Sir John Ross. They certainly do not in the slightest degree resemble those depicted in his voyage of 1819. Instead of being of the bright glaring crimson colour which they are represented to be in his plate, I could only make out in some places a brownish appearance, which seemed to be caused by the droppings of birds. We were within two miles of the cliffs, and as the day was brilliantly clear they could be seen with great distinctness. There was scarcely any snow on them. The want of this, its usual nidus, may account, perhaps, for the colour of the fungus, being less apparent at this time. I had noticed during our passage through the ice, that wherever the rotges (*Alca alle*) were, numerous of their droppings had a bright red appearance on the snow. Although it is now a well ascertained fact, that the cause of the colour of red snow is a vegetable organism (*Protococcus nivalis*), yet may not the dung of the little auk contain the germ thereof? This would seem to be the more likely, as the red snow has been only found on the cliffs which are the favourite brooding places of these birds.

To the northward of these cliffs are many glaciers, but of which, with my usual bad fortune, I could not get a closer view than from the deck with a telescope. Little can be said confidently as to the structure and formation of the icebergs without a thorough examination of these glaciers. But I will reserve the few unimportant facts that I have been able to observe with regard to icebergs for another chapter.

This was one of the most beautiful and delightful days we had as yet enjoyed since crossing the Arctic Circle, and we enjoyed it the more, seeing that during the whole month we had been amongst the ice of Melville Bay

it had been thick and misty. It was a dead
calm, and the very cliffs in shore were seen
mirrored on the water, the glassy smoothness
of which was unbroken, except by the plash-
ing of the oars from the long line of boats
ahead of each of the ships. The transpa-
rency of the atmosphere was such as can only
be conceived by those who have visited arctic
countries, and the whole scene was one that
it would be difficult to forget, the more so
since it was here we saw one of the most
beautiful icebergs of the many it was our
fortune to observe during the voyage. It was
of immense size. The south side, on which
we advanced towards it was almost perpen-
dicular, as if a recent split had taken place ;
but on rounding the corner and coming abreast
of the west side, which we did almost within
arm's-length, we found it to be wrought into
ledges,—ledge above ledge, each festooned with
a fringe of crystal icicles, which here and there
reaching the ledge beneath, formed columns
slender as those of a Saracenic mosque ; within
them ran a gallery green as emerald. Two or
three tiny cascades were tinkling from ledge
to ledge, and fell with a soft plash into the
water beneath, sending the pearl-like bubbles

dancing from them over the smooth surface. All was glancing and glittering beneath a bright sun, and if I had had it in my power I could have stood for hours to gaze at it. Passing the corner, the north side was seen to be cut into two deep little bays with sloping shores, a long point running out between them. The lowest ledge of the west side rounded the corner and inclined down towards the nearest bay, if so it may be called, and ending in a broad platform. This little bay seemed so snug, and lay so beautifully to the sun, that, unnatural as it may appear, one could not help fancying it,—as a fit site for a pretty cottage.

Loath to leave this fairy scene, even the slow progress the ship was making, towed by the weary arms of the crew, seemed by much too fast.

Almost all the bergs we saw here had similar beauties, though none were so remarkable as the one mentioned above. The ledges are formed by the under-wash of the sea at the floating line, each change of the position of the berg in the water adding to their number.

Continuing northwards, we passed Cape

Dudley Diggs. Opening Wolstenholm Sound, we sighted Dalrymple Rock, against which a few hours afterwards, thick weather coming on, one of our consorts made a narrow escape. We then struck out to the westward, and soon we were rejoiced to find that we could not be far from the " north water," as the ship began to " lift."

With a fine breeze, we could have now got on fast enough, but the thick weather delayed us somewhat amongst streams of ice. By the afternoon of the 4th we were fairly in the " north water," the ship again rising to the waves, and bounding cheerily to the westward before a fine breeze. We crossed to the southward of Carey's Islands in lat. 76° 30′, and saw the west land on the 8th.

CHAPTER IV.

POND'S BAY——WHALE HUNTING.

" I might here recreate your wearied eyes with an
hunting spectacle of the greatest chase which nature yieldeth, I mean, the killing of the whale.

" And thus they hold him in such pursuit, till after
streams of water, and next that of bloode, cast up into the
aire and water (as angry with both elements, which have
brought thither such weake hands to his destruction), he at
last yieldeth his slaine carkasse as meed to the conquerors."—PURCHASE'S *Pilgrimes*, 1626.

WE had a distant sight of the west coast
of Baffin's Bay, about lat. 76° N., on the
8th of July, being a part of North Devon.
We ran past the mouth of Lancaster Sound
with a strong breeze, and occasional heavy
squalls. The ice we passed during the day
was much heavier than any we had seen on
the east side, being apparently broken-up ice,
refrozen into tough solid masses, very un-
equal on the surface, and with deep over-

hanging edges, under which the sea was washing with a hollow dismal sound.

We were too distant at this time to make out whether or not the Sound was frozen across, but it may be believed it was not with uninterested eyes I looked in that direction, which, four years before, had been taken by those of whose welfare so many were now looking eagerly for tidings. I would fain have struck at once to the westward; however, there was nothing for it but to wait patiently. So I made up my mind to pass the next month in Pond's Bay as I best could, the hope never leaving me that I might yet succeed, one way or another, in getting up Lancaster Sound.

On the 9th we were reaching in to Cape Byam Martin, the snow-capped peaks of the Martin mountains towering up beyond. We ran rapidly to the southwards with a fine breeze, along the land ice past Cape Walter Bathurst.

In the evening we found ourselves off Cape Graham Moore, the northern point of Pond's Bay. It had now fallen almost a dead calm. Every one on board was on the alert and in high spirits, for as I have said before, the whalers consider that if they get to Pond's

Bay the first week in July, they are sure
to fall in with a run of whales and so
secure a full ship. The ship at this time
making scarcely head-way through the water,
the master was talking of sending the boats
into the bay, to see if they could fall in
with a fish or two. The deck was thronged
by the eager crew, the older hands pointing
out the well-remembered features of the bold
coast before them, each rendered memorable
in their eyes by the slaughter of some huge
" nine," or " ten footer," on former years.
In speaking of the size of a whale, they esti-
mate it by the length of the longest laminæ
of whalebone.

The harpooners were all busy in their boats,
examining their guns, harpoons, and lances ;
the attention of every one else was directed
towards the bay, when the sudden cries
of " A fish !" " A fish close astern !" " A
mother and sucker !" caused a rush to the
boats ; in an instant a couple were manned,
lowered, and after her. There she is—a large
whale, with the calf sporting about, and but
a short way astern ; the deep roust, and the
spouting fountain of her blast, contrasting with
the weaker and lower one of the calf. Ah!

they are down—the quick eye of the mother
has seen the boats, and she is off. The
faces around me on deck begin to elongate,
and their owners begin to think that it will
prove but a "loose fall" after all. But,
no ; the harpooner in the headmost boat is
a sharp fellow and an experienced—he has
marked which way the fish has "headed,"
and he is off after her, bending to his oar,
and urging his men to do the same, until
the boat seems to fly over the water For
twenty minutes they pull steadily on in the
same direction. Now, see ! the boat-steerer
is pointing ahead ; it is the calf that has risen
to breathe—had the poor mother been by
herself she would have been far enough by
this time, but she stays by her heedless offspring, and she now appears at the surface
also, within a "fair start" of the boat. A
few strong and steady strokes, and they are
at her. "He 's up! he has pushed out his
oar ; and stands to his gun." There is a
puff of smoke ; an instant afterwards a report
—the boat is enveloped in spray, and the
sea around broken into foam—as with an
agonised throe the mighty creature dives, in
the vain effort to escape. All this has been

witnessed from the ship with the most breathless anxiety; but now every soul is bawling "A fall!" "A fall!" at the pitch of their voices, whilst the rest of the crew are tumbling *pell-mell* into the remaining boats, which are lowered almost by the run, and without the loss of a second, are off towards the "fast one," which is now seen, with its "jack" flying, a happy sight to the master, who directs it to be replied to, by hoisting the ship's "jack" at the mizzen. The harpooneers in the loose boats now station themselves around the fast one, but at some distance from it, to be ready to attack the whale the moment she appears at the surface, with the exception of one which remains beside it to "bend on," should the fish take out all its lines.

Half an hour is now past, and during that time the fish has been "heading" towards the ship, so that the boats are but a short distance from us. Every instant she may be expected to reappear at the surface. "There she is!" "Hurrah boys!" "She spouts blood." The first harpoon has been well aimed, and sent home with deadly force; she is already far spent; but a second and a third are sent

crashing into her, and she dives again and
again, but for a shorter space each time, until
at last she lies almost motionless on the surface, whilst with the long and deadly lance
they search out her most vital parts. "Back!
back all of you! she's in her dying flurry."
No, she is too far spent, it is only a faint flap
of her heavy fin, and a weak lash of that tail
which, an hour back, could have sent all the
boats around her flying into splinters. She
turns slowly over on her side, and then floats
belly up, dead. "Three cheers, boys, for our
first Pond's Bay fish: I'se warrant ye, she's
eleven feet if she's an inch, and I'm sure
she's no been that ill to kill," cries out some
excited harpooner. The equally excited men
replying by three cheers of triumph that make
the blue bergs ring again.

But it must not be taken for granted that
the whale is always so easily captured as this
one was. It is often a work of severe labour,
and almost always one of considerable risk;
but the excitement of the sport is such, that
this is scarcely thought of. It is but seldom
now, however, that a whale can show much
fight, in consequence of the deadly effects of
the gun-harpoons, which are now constantly

used by all the ships. It may be easily conceived how much more efficacious these are
than the old hand-harpoons, particularly when
well aimed, and at a good range. A smart
harpooner, however, generally manages to get
fast with his hand-harpoon, as well as his gun,
being thus doubly secure of his fish.

All were of course highly encouraged at this
propitious beginning of the fishing, almost at
the very instant of our reaching the ground.
After " flensing " the whale, we proceeded in
to the land ice, and there made fast. On
coming into the bay we found a vessel lying
there, which turned out to be the " St. Andrew," of Aberdeen. We had many conjectures when we first saw her, whether it was
not the Investigator sent down here by Sir
James Ross to await our arrival. The " St.
Andrew " we found had got through the barrier of ice at the north end of Disco, *inside*, or
to the eastward of Hare Island, and proceeding northward, had found open water, almost
the whole way through Melville Bay, during
the beginning of June. She was only once
obliged to cut a dock, and arrived in Pond's
Bay on the 10th of June. She had been lying
here for a whole month, had seen no whales,

and, with the exception of a few unicorns,
had killed nothing or done nothing. I was
annoyed at this, or rather at my own bad
fortune in our ship, not having got through
at the same time ; merely in consequence of
our not succeeding in getting through the
barrier of ice at Hare Island when we first
attempted it. It was thick weather at the
time, and the " St. Andrew " took the inside
of the island, whilst we tried the outside. She
succeeded, but we had to put back. The
result is seen ; she was at the west side of
Baffin's Bay a full month before any of the
other ships, and had little or no difficulty
in effecting it. This proves that Mr. Penny
is right, in the opinion he has so often ex-
pressed to me, that the earlier in June the
passage through Melville Bay is attempted,
the easier will it be effected. He has pointed
out to me that the prevailing winds during
the month of May and the beginning of
June, are from the north or north-east, and
that the effects of these are to drive the
ice to the southward, consequently slacken-
ing it in Melville Bay, and the northern
part of the " middle ice," and thus rendering
the passage through it easier during the earlier

part of the month of June, than it is about the
end of it : and that it is still more difficult
during July, from the prevailing winds then
being from the south and south-west, their
effect being to pack the ice into Melville
Bay. Going over every year from 1820, he
has shown to me that the earlier the passage
has been attempted, the easier it has been ;
and that if the whale ships have been delayed
to the southwards, from any of the many
causes which are apt to do so, they have
always had proportionate difficulty in effecting
their passage, according to the period in the
month of July, in which it was attempted.*
For instance, Sir John Franklin's ships, in
1845, were only crossing the Arctic Circle
at the time we were this year (1849) in the
" north water." And, in 1845, Sir John
Franklin's ships were met in Melville Bay,
beset, and still forty miles from the " north
water," by the whalers returning full from
Pond's Bay.

Here is the " North Star," too ; had she
been dispatched in time, she might have been

* And it will be found that very few of the expeditions
have ever been able to do anything during the first summer of their voyage, from being always too late in sailing.

at the mouth of Lancaster Sound by the middle of June or beginning of July at the latest. We now know that she was not there up to the 20th of August.

I was the more annoyed at our bad luck, seeing that if we had got through at the same time as the " St. Andrew," some advantage might have been taken of the additional time thus gained, to search for some information of the Expeditions. I am certain, at least, we should not have been lying idle. Mr. Penny had proposed a most feasible plan to me, and which I should have been delighted to have had in my power to execute. He knew there was an Esquimaux at Pond's Bay of the name of Toonick, with whom he was well acquainted, an intelligent fellow, and who could speak English well. Our plan was, that I should make a bargain with this man to accompany me as a guide from Pond's Bay to Navy Board Inlet. With a couple of sledges, the necessary number of dogs, and Esquimaux attendants, we thought this could have been easily done, and I yet regret that I had it not in my power to try it. Although we visited Navy Board Inlet a month afterwards, and found no trace of the Expedition

E

there, yet my time would have been as well
employed as on board ship, and if I had done
nothing else, I could have ascertained whether
or not there is a sea communication between
the two inlets, which seems exceedingly probable. However, we found upon inquiry from
the first natives who came off to us, that
Toonick and almost all the rest of the Esquimaux had proceeded up the country salmon-
fishing. Those who were left were all old men,
many of them afflicted with snow-blindness;
and the only stout young fellow we saw
appeared to be idiotical. We could make
nothing whatever out of him. Our scheme
was thus knocked on the head, much to my
disappointment, as I had looked forward to
it with great hopes. It was here, and at this
time, that the Esquimaux report of the Expeditions originated. Those natives whom I
myself saw and interrogated, all answered my
questions in the affirmative. But, from my
imperfect knowledge of the Esquimaux dia-
lect, I was necessarily obliged to put leading
questions, so that I placed little or no confidence in their answers. When we heard that
the natives had given information of the safety
and present position of the Expedition, we

were rather astonished, particularly at the minuteness with which many facts were stated; but we in a very short time found that, even in its passage through one ship, the report had changed features, and gathered importance wonderfully. It is needless to repeat those things which throw doubt upon the truth of this report. In different articles in the " Athenæum," I think it is shown satisfactorily that little confidence can be placed in it. But I think that the mere fact, that Sir James Ross, during the whole course of his voyage never saw a single Esquimaux, should prove that it is utterly without foundation. And I must say, the person cannot be blamed too highly, who, whilst on the spot, openly avowed his disbelief in this report, and yet on his return home spread it throughout the length and breadth of the land, raising high hopes in the breasts of hundreds, which, he was fully aware, would in a few days be dashed aside.

For the next ten days we continued our fishing, with varying success, occasionally casting off from the ice, and running a short way to the southward, as the whales seemed to be more or less plentiful. We were more generally astir during the night than during the

day, for it almost invariably happened that " a
fall ! " if called at all during the four-and-
twenty hours, would be about midnight or
after it ; then adieu to sleep for the next eight
hours at least. But there was little privation
in this, for I think there are few men who
having once seen the exciting scene of a whale
hunt, would for an instant prefer their beds to
the pleasure of seeing it again. For some days
we had scarcely seen any fish. A small strag-
gler would be seen occasionally, and was soon
dispatched by some one or other of the ships ;
but still there was nothing like a " run ; " and,
although we ourselves were at that time better
fished than our neighbours, yet we were not
getting on half fast enough for some of the
more impatient spirits. For my part, every
successive capture we made was a sort of disappointment to me, for the more we got, the
less chance was there of our getting up Lancaster Sound, my only aim and object. Still,
it was pleasant to see all around me happy
at every accession to the cargo, which was to
take comfort and happiness to many a fire-
side and family during the winter, and for
which all the poor fellows were toiling so hard.
But, in spite of my so far selfish feeling, I

am certain I was as keen and as eager as any one on board whenever the exciting cry of "A fish!" was heard, or the still more exciting and rousing one of "A fall!" and I managed more than once to be "in at the death," and take my share in the sport, as well as in a drenching shower-bath of hot and greasy blood.

It was late in the evening of a brilliantly clear and warm day—one of those days which but too seldom enliven this land of eternal ice and snow, and which, when they do happen, contrast so delightfully with the many days of dreary mist which the visitor of Arctic countries has to endure.

Two or three of the hands were lounging listlessly about the decks, all the watch being "on the bran" * in the boats, stationed along the edge of the ice, to which the ship was made fast, and the rest of the crew sound asleep in their berths. The master had just gone up to the crow's-nest, to take a look around him before turning in. He had not been there many minutes, before his quick and well-trained eye saw whales blowing beyond

---

* Boats and their crews stationed along the edge of the ice, on the look-out for whales, are said to be " on the bran."

a point of ice some ten miles' distant. The welcome news soon spread that the long-looked for "run" was at length in sight, and ere long every soul was astir and ready for the sport. The boats were immediately lowered, those in the "bran" were called along side, all their kegs filled with bread, beef, and water, and a small supply of grog given to each. The master was anxiously reiterating his orders to each of the harpooners; whilst some of the keenest of them were running up to the crow's-nest, and as they came down again were asserting that they saw the whales spouting like "steam-coaches, only far thicker." Most of the boats were now sent off to meet the "run;" but in a short time the whales, showing no inclination to come further into the bay, the rest were dispatched also, with orders to pull right out to them. I had no idea of remaining by the now almost deserted ship at a distance from the scene, so I proposed to go in the last boat, and, as we were short enough of hands, I had no difficulty in getting my offer accepted. We had a long pull before us, but the anticipation of the sport, the delightful calm of the evening, and the beauty of the scene around us, shortened the

distance wonderfully. Looking towards· the
land from which we were pulling, nothing could
be more beautiful than the immense extent of
high and mountainous coast that was stretched out before us, broken across, as it were, by
the opening of the bay, the whole variegated
in the most beautiful manner by the lichen-
coloured rocks, and the brown patches of vegetation appearing above the ground-work of
snow ; whilst half-way down the black precipitous crags of the shore hung a long filmy
riband of gauze-like mist, tinted with the
most delicate crimson by the level rays of the
midnight sun. The whole, too, seemingly so
close at hand, that more than once throughout the past day I had caught myself wonder-
ing at my laziness in not stepping across the
narrow boundary of ice which separated me
from the shore, until I recollected that the
apparent mile was nearly fifteen, and these
fifteen rendered unsafe by the decayed state of
the ice. Nothing could be more tantalizing
than this apparent propinquity, for, after
months of confinement to the greasy decks of
a whaler, it would have been an unspeakable
luxury to have set foot on shore again, or to
have been able to pluck even the simplest

moss or lichen of the scanty Flora of the shore before us. The longing that a landsman has to be on shore again, after a tedious sea-voyage, may be easily conceived; but to sail for hundreds of miles without being able to land, within an apparent stone's throw of a coast— desolate it may be, but still rich in gloomy grandeur of scenery,—creates a longing which it may well be believed is much more intense.

But we are now drawing nigh the scene of action; we had for some time been meeting numerous shoals of narwhals (*Monodon monoceros*), whose blasts every now and then startled us, as they are almost as loud as that of the whale.*

We passed a Kirkaldy vessel, the crew of which were busily engaged, and pulling onwards; we shortly came up to one of our own boats, which we found had succeeded in killing a large fish of ten or eleven feet bone: the fish was floating at the edge of the floe, and the boat's crew would fain have had ours to join them in the laborious and irksome task of hauling in their lines. But we had no idea of this when there was sport to participate in

* The whalers have a saying, "after seals unies, after unicorns whales."

a little farther on : so, after a few minutes
spent in asking questions, how many lines she
had taken out, &c., all of which seem so interesting to the true whaler, we had regained
breath, and pulled onwards. About three
miles further on we found a second boat with
her "jack" flying, denoting that she was fast.
Passing close to this boat, we found that the
fish was taking out line with great force and
rapidity, and that the harpooner was rather
doubtful as to his being "well fast" or not;
that is to say, he was uncertain whether
his harpoon was securely inserted into the
whale ; he had fired at a long range just as the
fish was going down. We pulled in the direction in which she was "heading," where the
rest of the boats already were ; before we got
up to them, she had made her appearance at
the surface; a second boat had got fast to her,
and just in time, as she was seen to be "loose"
from the first. She did not take out much
line from this boat, but remained away a
considerably longer time than usual, greatly
to our astonishment, until we found that she
was "blowing" in some holes in the floe, a
good distance from the edge of it. One of the
harpooners immediately proceeded over the ice

with a hand-harpoon, trailing the end of the
line with him, assisted by part of his crew,
and from the edge of the hole drove his weapon
into the body of the poor whale; whilst some
of the others following plied the bleeding
wretch with their long lances, so that she was
soon obliged to betake herself again to the
open water outside the floe.   Here more of
her enemies were waiting, for our boat was
immediately upon her, and a gun-harpoon was
at once driven almost out of sight into her
huge side, which was already bristling with
weapons.   Our boat was on her very back as
she dived, with an unwieldy roll, which sent
it surging gunwale under, taking the line
whistling out for a score fathoms, until the
harpooner, knowing she was pretty well exhausted, stopped her way, by taking three
or four turns round the "bollard."   But
every few seconds she would make a start,
drawing the boat almost head under, until
the line was permitted to run out again,
which, as it did so, made a grinding, burring
noise, eating deep into the hard lignum vitæ
of the bollard, enveloping the harpooner in
smoke, and causing the most distinct smell
of burning, which was only prevented from

actually taking place by the line-manager throwing water constantly on it.

Again she appeared at the surface, but far exhausted, still she made a strong fight for it, lashing about with her tail and fins in fury whenever she seemed to have regained breath. It was no very pleasant sight to see her tail quivering high up in the air, within but a short distance of us, and coming down on the water with a loud sharp crack, like the report of a dozen rifles, and which, had it alighted on any of our boats, had power sufficient to have converted their timbers into something very like lucifer matches. A few more lances soon settled her, and ere long she was rolling on her back. The usual cheers of triumph were given, and we had time to breathe and shake ourselves, for it may be believed we had not escaped the showers of spray which the defunct had sent about so liberally.

The water far around us was dyed with blood and covered with a thick pellicle of oil, upon which the Mollys were as busy as they could be, whilst the edges of the ice, as far as we could see, were deeply crimsoned; and a hummock on the edge of the floe, beside

which the final struggle had taken place, was
from the summit downwards streaked with
the black blood which the last few blasts of
the dying monster had sent over it.

Much to our satisfaction, we had little line
to pull in, so that we were soon ready for
another victim. It must not be thought,
however, that I have been all this time an
idle spectator. If one wishes to partake in
this sport he must also partake in the labour.
The whale-boats are necessarily so constructed
that they can only contain their proper crew.
But as I was able to handle an oar, from
former practice, I had no difficulty in finding
a place in them, and so gaining a closer view
of the scene. The labour was severe, as we
had already pulled upwards of fifteen miles,
and that at full stretch, as hard as we could
lay to our oars; but this was scarcely thought
of at the time. It was only now when the
excitement was over that I thought of fatigue
or felt it. I had luckily pitched my pea-
jacket into the boat when we left the ship,
as I had a sort of idea we might be some
time away, so I now rolled it up, placed it
on the gunwale of the boat, and stretching
myself out on the " thwart," slept as soundly

as ever I did in my life. My slumbers, however, did not last long, for it was scarcely
according to rule that any one should sleep
in the boats on fishing-ground. But I woke
thoroughly refreshed, and we were again in
full chase after the "fish."

We had two or three unsuccessful bursts
after them, but failed in getting within
striking distance. We saw one of the boats,
however, a short way from us fire at a large
fish, which, on receiving the harpoon, leapt
almost clean out of the water, head first,
displaying the greater part of its huge bulk
against the sky, until we thought it was going
to jump right on to the floe. Suddenly re-
versing itself, its tail was seen high over the
boat, and so near that for an instant or two
we breathlessly expected to hear the cry of
agony from the poor fellows as they were
crushed beneath it. But she dived sheer
downwards, quite clear of the boat, towards
which we now pulled quickly to render assistance, more excited, perhaps, by the narrow
escape we had just witnessed than they were
themselves. Distant as we were from the
ship, and notwithstanding the hairbreadth
escape they had just made, the joyous shout

of "A fall!" was now raised, and the Jack displayed. Just, however, as we reached it, the line which had for the few seconds since the fish had dived been running out with lightning speed, slackened, and the strain stopped. The harpooner looked blue, and began slowly hauling in, his crew assisting, with long faces; for, be it remarked, each man in a "fast boat" gets half-a-crown and the harpooner half-a-guinea. We sat gravely by, condoling with them on having lost their fish. In a few minutes the harpoon appeared on the surface, and was hauled on board, with sundry maledictions from the *heathens* of the unlucky boat. The whale had wrenched herself loose by her sudden and active leap, for the massive iron shaft of the harpoon was bent and twisted upon itself as one would twist a piece of soft copper-wire with a pair of pliers.

We pulled back again towards our former station. By this time we scarcely knew whether it was night or day. We had a sort of idea that we had been a night and a day away from the ship, but of that we were not certain. We had made repeated attacks upon the biscuits and canister of preserved meats,

but although the appetites of steady-living
people at home are pretty fair time-keepers,
we found ours of little use in that way here.

I suspected it was again night, but I could
scarcely think it possible, the time seemed to
have passed so rapidly. But there was a *stillness* about the air that must have struck every
one as peculiar to the dead hour of the night,
and although I have noticed it in far different
situations, it never struck me so forcibly as it
did here. The light passing breezes and cats'
paws which had dimpled the water for some
hours back had died away. It was now so
calm that a feather dropt from the hand fell
plumb into the sea. But it was the dead stillness of the air which was so peculiar. No hum
of insect, none of the other pleasant sounds
which betoken it is day, and that Nature is
awake, can be expected here even at midday
in the height of summer, twenty miles from
land, and that land far within the Arctic
Circle, where, if one may say so, a third of the
year is one long continuous day. Yet there is
a most perceptible difference,—there is a stir
in the air around,—a sort of *silent music* heard
during day which is dumb during night. Is
it not strange that the deep stillness of the

dead hour of night should be as peculiar to
the solitude of the icy seas as to the centre
of the vast city? For many hours we lay
quietly still, no fish coming near enough for
us to attempt getting fast. But during the
whole of this time they were pouring round
the point of ice, and apparently running in
towards the bay, almost in hundreds. The
deep boom of their blowings, resounding
through the still air, like the distant bellowing of a herd of bulls. My ear should have
been pretty well accustomed now to the blast
of the whales, but it was not until this
time that I ever had noticed the peculiar
hollow *boom* of their voice, if voice it may
be called.

We thought at the time that the fish were
running right into the bay, and imagined we
could hear the distant sound of the guns,
and the shouting of "falls" about the ships,
which could just be seen. We were in no
very good humour at the idea of not being
in the thick of it, but we had no reason to
complain as it turned out, for we learned,
on our return, that the fish had never gone
into the bay, and that scarcely any one had
seen them on this occasion but ourselves.

But we now had a good chance ; a fish was seen beside the ice at no great distance from us, but beyond a "fair start." I have noticed a peculiarity about the whale, that if there is a piece of ice within sight it will run towards it, and come to the surface beside it. And when beside a floe it always rises beside its edge, and never appears at any distance from it. And, moreover, if there should be a crack or bight in the floe, it is ten chances to one it will rise to blow in it, in preference to the outer edge of the floe. This is well known to the whalers. Such a crack being now opposite to us, and at such a distance from where the whale was last seen, it was likely she would rise there next, and we pulled towards it. Here we lay for some minutes in breathless expectation, our oars out of the water, and the harpooner silently motioning with his hand to the boat-steerer which way to "scull." Up in the very head of the crack the water was now seen to be circling and gurgling up, "There's her eddy," quietly whispers our harpooner : "A couple of strokes now, boys,—gently,— that'll do." Looking over my shoulder, I could see first the crown, then the great black

back of the unsuspecting whale, slowly emerge
from the water, contrasting strangely with
the bright white and blue of the ice on each
side—then followed the indescribable hurstling
roar of her blast. But short breathing time
had she—for, with sure aim and single tug
of his trigger-string, the keen iron was sent
deep in behind her fin. "*Harden up, boys!*"
he cries, and the boat is pulled right on to
the whale, when he plunges the hand-harpoon
deep into her back, with two hearty *digs*.
The poor brute quivered throughout, and for
a second or two lay almost motionless; then
diving, and that with such rapidly increasing
speed, that the line was whirled out of the
boat like lightning. The usual signals were
now made to the other boats that we were
"fast."

For the first few minutes the lines were
allowed to run out without interruption, then,
one, two, three turns, were successively
thrown round the "bollard." This had the
effect of stopping her speed somewhat, but
the line still ran out with a great strain.
The boat's bow was forcibly pressed against
the ice, and crushed through the underwashed
ledge, to the solid floe beyond; the harpooner

sitting upon his "thwart," allowing the lines
to run through his hands, which were defended
by thick mitts : stopping the progress of the
fish as much as he could, as the rest of the
boats were still some distance from us. Every
few minutes the fish seeming to start off as
with renewed strength, the boat's bow would
be pulled downwards, threatening to pull us
bodily under the floe. But then allowing
the line to run out, the strain was partly
removed, and the boat's head again rose, but
only to be again dragged downwards. Upwards of twenty minutes had elapsed since
we had "got fast," and the strain now began
to slacken, but it was full time,—we were
drawing nigh the "bitter end." The welcome
sound of a gun was heard, and in a few
seconds, looking down the edge of the floe
we could see one of our boats with the well-
known blue "Jack" flying. A few fathoms
more of line were rapidly drawn out, and
then the strain as suddenly ceased. We commenced hauling them in, and whilst doing
so, could see a third boat "get fast." The
rest of the boats were now at hand, and as
she appeared at the surface, closely surrounded
her, and busily plied her with their lances.

It was in about an hour and a half from the time we first struck her, that we heard the distant cheers announcing her death. From the time the second boat had got fast we had been busily engaged hauling in our lines, and thus slowly approaching the cluster of boats round the dying whale. But long ere we had finished this they had succeeded in killing her, and she was lying safe and sound, made fast to the edge of the floe. The boats now collected and prepared to tow the dead fish to the ship. This was even more tedious than hauling in the lines, but as I had volunteered to take my place in a boat, I said not a word, but tugged away at my oar in silence. Luckily, however, one or two fish were seen near us, in pursuit of which our boat and another cast off from those which were towing. The moment we were again in chase, fatigue and languor vanished, and we stretched to our oars as heartily as we had done when we first left the ship.

We had a long, but a fruitless pull, and in the mean time a light breeze had sprung up, and we could see that the ship had "cast off" from the land ice in the bay, and was working down towards the boats and dead fish. We pulled towards her at once, and I was not a little glad to be able to stretch myself on deck again, after nearly forty-eight hours confinement to the thwart of a boat. A hearty welcome from the captain, who was not a little astonished to find me so fresh after my labours, and the tempting sight of smoking beef-steaks and *early potatoes** on the cabin table, soon made me all right, nor did I feel half so fatigued as I might have expected, and was later than even my usual time of retiring to my narrow berth in the

* It may appear rather strange that we should have early potatoes on board ship within the Arctic circle, but for upwards of three months, from June to September, we had every day more than a quart of them at dinner. A large supply of excellent potatoes had been put on board at Dundee, a good deal of mould being amongst them, and the place where they were stored being not far from the stove, and under the water, they had sprouted and formed young tubers. The Steward having informed us of this, orders were given that he should be careful in removing the daily supply, and rather to encourage than interfere with the growth of this unlooked-for delicacy. They were about as large as a pigeon's egg, and exceedingly good—better, indeed, than forced early potatoes at home. As I am upon the subject of eatables, I may mention that the Captain and I not unfrequently indulged in a broiled whale steak and broiled whale skin, both of which are very fair eating indeed, and which, if it came to be a matter of necessity, I should think excellent.

little closet off the cabin, which was by courtesy
termed the *Doctor's state-room*.

Two or three days after this, I had another
opportunity of closely witnessing the death
of a whale. She had been struck in a crack
but a short distance from the ship. All the
crew, except the "watch," who were on the
"bran," were sound asleep in their berths
below, fatigued after some days' hard labour.
It is a most laughable scene to see a "fall
called" under such circumstances. The one
or two hands, who were walking quietly and
gently on deck a second before, in order
not to disturb the fatigued men below, are
now seen dancing and jumping like madmen,
on the half-deck hatch, screaming "a fall!"
as if for their lives. The more active men
of the crew are on deck in an instant, with
ready bundle of clothes in hands, and shoes
or boots slipped loosely on their feet. But
it is generally a race who will be first into
their boats, clothed or unclothed, and nothing
is more common than to see half a dozen
fellows rushing to the boats with nothing
on but their woollen under-clothing, the rest
in a bundle under their arm, trusting to the
first stoppage to complete their toilette, such

as it is. Rather a sudden change this from
their close and crowded "bunks" (as they
call them) in the half-deck, to an atmosphere
often far below zero. But neither the old
whaling sailor, nor the green Orkney boy,
ever seemed to feel it.

The stern-boat was the only one now left
on board. The master ordering it to be
lowered, and getting into it himself, I jumped
in with him. We pulled up to the "fast
boat," to see how things were getting on,
and found they were only fast with the gun-
harpoon, and not very well with that. Whilst
talking to the harpooner of this boat, we
heard a commotion amongst the others, and
almost before we had time to turn, bang!
went one of their guns, and the fish was
made almost secure. She seemed to dive
under the floe, and reappeared almost at the
same place, for she next came up within a
very short distance of where she was first
struck, when a third boat got fast to her,
and before she dived again she was mortally
lanced. When she next appeared at the
surface, it was close to our boat; we were
at her in a minute, when the ready lance
of the master was twice buried deep behind

her fin. She made a rush forwards, which pulled the lance out of his hand, but he soon had a second—we "hardened up" to the fish, when he plunged it into her side. She had been quiet enough hitherto, but it was now full time for him to cry, "Back, men, for your lives!" I heard a sudden whizzing, whistling sound in the air—I thought a black cloud had passed between us and the sun —a drenching shower of spray passed over us, and there was a loud *thud* upon the water on the other side of the boat, as her huge tail descended into the sea, which it continued to lash into seething foam for more than five minutes. It may be believed that whilst this was going on we all kept at a safe distance. It was, however, only the last struggle—"the dying flurry," and the huge mass was soon lying powerless and motionless before us. This was a female whale, and one of the largest we had yet seen. Her bulk may be imagined from the following measurement, which I managed to take whilst she was fastened alongside, previous to the commencement of "flensing." *

* Measurements of a female whale killed in Pond's Bay, on the 17th of July, 1849 :—

With such stirring sights as these, of almost
daily occurrence, it may be imagined that the
time would seldom hang heavy on my hands,
yet my object in being here at all rarely
left my mind; and now, as fish after fish
added to the extent and value of our cargo,
my hopes of being able to get up Lancaster
Sound, began to wax fainter and fainter.

Length from the fork of the tail along the abdomen
    to the tip of the lower jaw, ... 65 feet
Girth behind the fins (Kant slip), .   .   . 30 „
Breadth of tail from tip to tip, .   .   . 24 „
Greatest breadth between lower jaws, . . 10 „
Length of head, measuring to a line from articula-
    tion of lower jaw, ... 21 „
Length of vulva, ... 14 inc.
From posterior end of vulva to anus, .   . 6 „
From anterior end of vulva to umbilicus, . 8 feet
Mammæ opposite the anterior third of vulva, and 6
    inches from tip of it.
Length of sulcus of mammæ 3 inches, sulcus on
    each side of it 2 inches.
From the tuberosity of humerus to point of fin, . 8 feet
Greatest breadth of fin, ... 3 ft. 11 in.
Depth of lip (interior lower). .   .   . 4 „ 7 „
From inner canthus of the eye to extreme angle of
    fold of the mouth, ... 17 inc.
From inner to outer canthus, .   .   . 6 „
Length of the block of laminæ of baleen, measuring
    round the curve of the gum, after removal from
    the head, ... 16 ft. 6 in.

F

However, on the 1st of August, we heard
of the Esquimaux report, which I noted down
as follows, almost verbatim from Mr. Parker's
account of it : —

" We, this morning, had what might have
been considered as cheering intelligence of
' the Franklin Expedition ;' Mr. Parker, the
master of the ' Truelove,' of Hull, came on
board to breakfast, and informed us that
some Esquimaux, who had been on board
the ' Chieftain,' of Kirkaldy, had sketched

Length of longest lamina of each side, . 10 ft. 6 in.
Between the laminæ at the gum ⅛th of an inch.
Breadth of pulp cavity of largest lamina, . . 1 „
Average length of pulp when extracted from some
    of the largest lamina, ... 5 „
Number of laminæ of each side about 360.

The longest laminæ about the middle, their length gradually decreasing from behind forwards, and from before
backwards, their inner edge fringed with long coarse hair,
and their outer sharpened to an edge is bent backwards,
each lamina thus overlapping its neighbour, and giving the
series of plates the appearance of a Venetian blind. Many
of the laminæ are beautifully variegated by alternate longi-
tudinal streaks of black and white. I think I could make
out that the laminæ of the female whale are shorter, but
broader than those of the male.

The above measurements are necessarily imperfect; it
was impossible to ascertain the length along the curve of
the back, besides other points of interest, but I hope the
difficulties that lay in my way will prove my excuse.

a chart, and pointed out to Mr. Kerr where both Sir John Franklin's and Sir James Ross' ships were lying, the former being at Whaler Point, the latter at Port Jackson, at the entrance to Prince Regent's Inlet. Sir John Franklin had been beset in his present position for three winters. Sir James Ross had travelled in sledges from his own ship to Sir John Franklin's. They were all alive and well. The Esquimaux himself had been on board all the four ships three moons ago, *i. e.*, about the end of April, or the beginning of May. Mr. Parker seemed confident as to the correctness of this information, and as his ship is nearly full, and he will proceed homewards very shortly, Mr. Kerr had given him the chart, which he said he intended to forward to the Admiralty, and inform them of what he had learned." Although, as I have formerly explained, we saw much to throw doubt upon this report, yet it was so far good, that it would in all likelihood induce one or more of the vessels to proceed towards the Sound.

CHAPTER V.

At last, after months of hopes, fears, and disappointments, we are fairly under weigh for Lancaster Sound. God grant we may see or hear something of Sir John Franklin's ships! but if this Esquimaux report does turn out true, and they are still at the mouth of Prince Regent's Inlet, the idea that they have got no further than this during *four* seasons, will be almost as annoying to them, as not hearing of them at all will be to us.

The more I think of the report, the less faith am I inclined to place in it; yet it may well be conceived how delighted I am to find the "Old Advice" running smartly towards Lancaster Sound. My long cherished hopes will now, I trust, be fulfilled.

Early on the 2nd we heard what we had guessed before, of the loss of the "Lady Jane" of Newcastle, and the "Superior" of Peterhead.

The American ship "MaClellan" brought
this piece of intelligence, and she had herself
been much damaged by the ice. Not a word
was there of the "North Star," and I now
begin to think it will be extremely doubtful whether or not she will ultimately get
through.

Had she only sailed in time, she might have
got through Melville Bay, along with the
fleet of whalers with the greatest ease, and
have had it in her power to proceed up Lancaster Sound early in July, or at least as
soon as the ice broke up.

However, here we are ourselves, off Cape
Walter Bathurst, with a fine breeze from the
S.S.E. Throughout the night a strong and
favourable breeze continued to carry us rapidly
into the Sound, the weather still keeping clear
and delightful. A keen and anxious look-out
was kept by all those on deck for the slightest
trace which might have been left by either of
the expeditions. We had run past the magnificent headland of Cape Byam Martin, and
Possession Bay was opening out to our view.
It still continued beautifully clear, but every
object within sight was transformed by refraction—a phenomenon, the effects of which

so often attract the attention of the Arctic
voyager.

A long point of ice stretched out ahead.
I was standing on the forecastle, examining
with a telescope every part of the shore with
an anxious eye, when with a thrill of joy I
recognised a flag-post and ensign. I gazed
earnestly at it; there could be no mistake;
I could almost make out the waving of the
flag. Without saying a word I put the glass
into the hands of a man who was standing
near me, and told him to look at the point
ahead. He did so, and with a start, immediately exclaimed that he saw a signal flying.
Delighted and overjoyed I snatched the glass
from his hands, and again applied it to my
eyes. For an instant I saw the wished-for
signal, but for an instant only—it faded, and
again appeared, but now distorted into a
broken and disjointed column, now into an
upturned and inverted pyramid. The refraction had caused a hummocky piece of
ice to assume these forms.*

* This chapter appeared in the "Morning Herald" of
23rd December last. The paragraph above, referring to
the illusive flag-post, elicited communications from more
than one authority on these subjects. They seemed to

I need not attempt to explain the sudden elevation I experienced at this moment, still less the worse depression I had to undergo when I found my fond hopes were dashed aside. Still I resumed my eye search along the shore, as did also not a few warm-hearted souls on board, the master scarcely ever leaving the crow's nest.

During the whole of Friday, the 3rd, a favourable breeze continued to carry us rapidly on. We had as yet seen very little ice, and what we had seen was very light: everything looked well, and we had high hopes.

think that I was wrong in taking it for granted that it was merely the effects of refraction, and that, in fact, there might have been a real signal. This arose from my careless wording of the paragraph, which might lead one to conceive that what I saw was on a point of *land*, whereas it was on a point of *ice*, where it was exceedingly unlikely, if not impossible, that any signal could be planted. There was no land *right a head*, in which direction I saw the signal; and although there are many well-authenticated instances of vessels and other objects being seen from an immense distance from the effects of refraction, yet, as far as I am aware, and from what little I know of the laws of refraction, there has been no instance of an object being refracted at *right* angles from its position, in which direction this must have been refracted—taking for granted that a signal would only be planted on *terra firma*, and from the relative position of the ship and the land at the time.

Whilst off Cape Hay, an Admiralty cylinder was put overboard, enclosed in a large cask, according to the Admiralty instructions, marked with a pole and vane, and properly ballasted. Though we were going at a great rate, we saw it distinctly nearly three-quarters of an hour afterwards; the red vane on the long pole being very conspicuous. I need not tell of our feelings at this time, or of our hopes, that this might meet the eyes of those for whom it was intended. Whilst running past Navy-board Inlet, a sudden shift of the wind forced us to stand more to the northward, so that we could make out the headlands of the opposite shore, looming through the distance.

The shore on the south side, as far as I could make out, seemed to be of a much leveller and flatter appearance than any parts of the coast I had hitherto seen. The immense towering and snow-capped mountain ranges had disappeared, and a moor-like champaign country taken their place. On some parts of the shore, however, were abruptly precipitous rocks, of a remarkable appearance, perfectly flat on the top, and having a basaltic buttressed look in front. They had none of that stratified appearance which all the rocky shores we have hitherto seen have had. However, as I can scarcely say yet that I have been on shore, I have, therefore, no title to say anything whatever decidedly of the geological formations of the country. But the snow lodging in the successive ledges of the Trap Rocks, is apt to deceive one into the idea of their stratification, despite one's knowledge of their peculiar cleavage. Nothing strikes one more, than the alternate " *ebon and ivory* " which marks the face of the towering cliffs of this country.

We continued running, with every sail set that would draw, during the whole of Friday the 3rd. Late in the evening it began to lower and overcast, when I retired to my berth, having been on deck without intermission, since we entered the Sound. On going on deck again at 4 A.M., the 4th, to my great chagrin I found that it was quite thick, and blowing very hard, with a heavy sea, and all the appearance of an increasing gale. The top-gallant-sails had to be stowed, and the top-sails reefed. By six A. M. the gale had so increased that the ship had to be hove-to under close reefed main-top-sail. A heavy

cross sea was by this time running, and it
was exceedingly thick and misty. At ten A.M.
we fell in with heavy washing ice; a press
of sail had to be made on the ship, and she
was reached over to the north side of the
Sound, where she was again hove-to, until ten
at night, when the ice was again found to
be under our lee. The sea was here breaking
with the greatest violence and magnificence
upon the heavy masses of ice, and upon a
solitary berg which was in sight.

Sail had again to be made, and the ship
plied to windward. A very heavy cross sea
running, the waist boats were taken in on
deck. It moderated slightly on the forenoon
of Sunday; the sea was falling, and to my
great joy the weather began to clear. We
found ourselves in a deep bight of the ice,
which apparently stretched in a crescentic or
concave direction, from Cape York on the
south side to about Burnett's Inlet on the
north. The gale had completely broken up
the ice, that is to say it was in the state of
pack ice. Mr. Penny saw Prince Leopold's
Island from the mast-head, and moreover he
distinctly saw a water sky* beyond.

* "Water-sky." A certain dark appearance of the sky,

I could not but have the most perfect confidence in this opinion of Mr. Penny's, for I knew that he had an eye thoroughly educated to the use of the telescope, and, as I have on many occasions had opportunities of remarking, is an adept in the use of it.

All hopes of proceeding further had now to be given up, and we at once commenced to ply our way out of the Sound, deeply chagrined at having to renounce our search. For my own part, I was miserably distressed ; I had failed in achieving the only object of my voyage. But Mr. Penny had scarcely another course open to him ; he was not authorised to prosecute the search, or to go out of his way in obtaining information regarding the expeditions. As long as there was a chance of procuring whales in Prince Regent's Inlet,* he might have persevered,

which indicates clear water in that direction, and which, when contrasted with the blink over ice or land, is very conspicuous.—PARRY.

* A leading morning paper, in different articles which have of late appeared in it, seems to doubt that any benefit has accrued to the country from the various Arctic expeditions. To say nothing of the immense amount of scientific knowledge that has been gained through them, I may merely state, that the value of the whales captured

deep as his ship was in the water, and great
as the risk would have been in pushing
through the heavy pack-ice we had fallen in
with. But when, at the conclusion of the
gale, we found that the land ice had been
entirely broken up, which rendered it impossible to prosecute the fishing in this direction,
and consequently his continuation of a search
after the expeditions incompatible with his
duty to his owners, he was reluctantly com-
pelled to retrace his steps.*

The next three days were melancholy
enough; we were now retracing our steps;
there was no hope of future success to sustain
us now. The weather, too, was cloudy, dark,
and stormy. Our progress eastward was very
slow—a curious fact, as on former occasions
the difficulty always has been to make their

in Navy Board, Admiralty, and Prince Regent's, Inlets,
since their discovery by Parry, would more than pay the
expense of all the expeditions from that time up to Sir
John Franklin's. May we not hope then that the present
expedition may be the means of further stimulating and
encouraging commercial enterprise.

* It may easily be conceived how annoying it was, on
the return of Sir James C. Ross, but a few days after our
own arrival, to find that we had been so short a distance
from him.

way up the Sound against the current which
sets to the eastward with great strength.

About mid-day on Thursday, the 9th, it
began to clear. We found ourselves about
three miles off the west point of Navy Board
Inlet. Throughout the afternoon and evening it gradually improved until about midnight, when it was calm and brilliantly clear.
An Admiralty cylinder was now got ready
and enclosed in a small cask, along with some
of the latest newspapers which we had on
board. I debated long with myself whether
or not I should inclose letters to Harry; but
when I recollected that the bad news I should
have to communicate would more than coun-
terbalance the good—that the intelligence of
the loss of more than one near and dear relative during his long absence, would give
infinite pain, and that, perhaps, at a time
when every man of them would require to
be sustained rather than depressed, I refrained
from expressing my feelings as a brother,
trusting, that if they did fall in with our
deposit, it would show them that their friends
and fellow-countrymen were not unmindful
of their welfare. Two boats were dispatched
on shore to bury the cask in the most con-

spicuous place possible. I went in one of
them. After about two hours hard pulling
we landed on the nearest island, on the west
side of the inlet — one of the Wollaston
Islands, I apprehend. Whilst pulling in and
approaching the land, it may be believed that
I strained my eyes in search of cairns or
signals of any sort, but not the slightest
vestiges of such were to be seen. As we
rounded the west side of the island, to obtain
a suitable landing place, I saw many blocks
of ice aground, and observed through the clear
water that the rocks at the bottom were all
scratched and polished by the friction of the
ice. The only appearance of algæ were in
the deep clefts of the rocky bottom, and
these were but scanty. We landed on the
south-west side of the island, and found it
to be entirely composed of limestone, and
about little more than a quarter of a mile
square. We ascended at once to its highest
point, where the men began to dig a hole
for the cask. I then hurriedly walked round
the island, and found scattered about on it
many large worn boulders of granite, some of
them more than half way up to the highest
point, which I should say was about fifty or

sixty feet above the level of the sea. There
was scarcely any vegetation to be seen; two
species of grasses, and a saxifrage (*Saxifraga
appositifolia*) were all that I could gather.
We disturbed, on our landing, about a
dozen eider-ducks (*Somateria mollissima*). Their
eggs I found to be within a very few hours of
maturity. I saw none of the male eider-duck,
all those seen were females. There were numerous nests, the occupants of which had,
I suppose, already winged their way southwards. We saw two Brent geese (*Anser berni-
cla*), and a single pair of Arctic terns (*Sterna
arctica*), the last of which were most vociferous and courageous in defence of their
downy offspring whenever I approached their
nest. These were the only birds I saw, with
the exception of a solitary raven (*Corvus
corax*) hovering high overhead, whose sharp
and yet musically bell-like croak came start-
ling upon the ear.

On the east side of the island, in a snugly
sheltered little cove, were the remains of an
Esquimaux summer hut, but evidently of some
seasons back; surrounded by the bones of
the bear, fox, and seal, and a few little bits
of baleen. I observed also a portion of the

base of a human skull, but evidently long exposed to the effects of weather and atmosphere.

In the mean time the men had buried the cask, a cairn of stones was erected over the spot, and a pole erected thereon, on which was fastened a black ball.

We then prepared to return to the " Advice," which by this time had stood further in, and had the signal of recall hoisted. It was with slow and tardy steps that I made my way towards the boats, scarcely being able to believe it was necessary I should leave a spot which seemed to me so near our dear friends—a spot, moreover, rendered memorable as being almost the exact one from which a well nigh despairing party was, on a former occasion, snatched from a lingering fate.*

We had not been long on board before thick weather came on. We lost sight of the land entirely, and standing right to the westward for two days, did not see it again until we were far to the southward, in lat. 71° 59'.

Hitherto there had been something to sus-

* It was near this place that Sir John Ross and his party were picked up by the "Isabella" of Hull, in 1834.

tain us, but now that we had turned our
backs on Lancaster Sound, now, when all
hopes of hearing aught of them, or being
able to render any assistance had vanished,
I was wretched enough; but, "Hope's blest
dominion never ends," and soon she began
to whisper to me, "They will have got
through; they will be home as soon as you
will; they have solved the long-doubtful pro-
blem of the north-west passage, which will
certainly be much more gratifying to all parties, than if they had to retrace their steps,
disappointed and discomfited. Soon, therefore,
I began to regain spirits, and become recon-
ciled to the bad success of my voyage.

We made the land again about Agnes'
Monument, but I got but a distant and in-
distinct view of this remarkable headland.
The coast to the southward presented the
same features we had for months been accustomed to. There was somewhat less snow
on the mountains; they appeared, if anything,
blacker and gloomier than what we had hitherto
seen. I should have liked exceedingly to land
here, but had no chance of doing so. One
of the mates greatly excited my curiosity
and desire to land, by his tales about the ex-

cellent sport that has been had here by many
of the whalers in rein-deer shooting. He also
told me that he had, when they landed,
always captured great numbers of " big mice,"
as he called them, " with fine long fur."
Some species of lemming this must be, I suppose. I learned now, also, that fossil fish
have been found on the east side of Baffin's
Bay, both in the Island of Disco and the
coast to the northward. At, least I heard
from this same man that " stone fish " had
been there found, and that a few had been
taken home as curiosities by some of the
whaling captains.

What a rich store for the Paleontologist
there may yet be in the more accessible parts
of the coasts of Greenland and Labrador!
I never had an opportunity of procuring any
of these fossils ; and, in fact, the whole voyage
was a failure to me, as far as Natural History
was concerned ; it was too successful in whaling
to allow of much to be done.

The Naturalist, if he takes his chance in
a whaling voyage, will find that he will be
able to do little, if the voyage is successful
as a whaling voyage ; but if, on the contrary,
it is " a bad year," in whaler parlance, then

there is little to prevent him from reaping
a rich harvest. I had every assistance possible from Mr. Penny, but from my own in-
experience, I am afraid I lost not a few opportunities of observation. You may recollect
the story of John Hunter's sending out a
surgeon specially to Greenland to make a
collection for him, and that at not a little
expense—of his chagrin when the man returned with a collection consisting of a piece
of whale's skin, to which were attached some
of the whale louse (*Oniscus ceti*), and nought
else. But I much suspect that the man
need not be so much laughed at. Ten chances
to one, he was with people who would laugh
and sneer at his every effort, and throw difficulties in his way that he would not have it
in his power to surmount. I was not thus
situated myself, but I saw and heard quite
sufficient to show me that the position of
surgeon of a whale ship is no very enviable
one, and too often, I am sorry to say, rendered
worse, from their own mismanagement.

We continued working our way southwards,
running a considerable way into Home Bay.
I was informed that a strong current is always
found setting into this inlet, and as it has

never yet been examined, I should not be
at all astonished to find that it may communicate with Fox's Channel, or Fury and
Hecla Straits.

We captured one middling-sized whale off
this bay, and then slowly worked our way
southwards. For some time we saw nothing
worthy of notice or comment. A little to the
southward of this, however, a few days afterwards, we fell in with a "*run*" of fish. It
was about mid-day, the water was very free
of ice, and a good deal of sea was running,
there being a sharp breeze. Three of the
boats were lowered, and they had a pretty
good tossing about for some hours, but were
completely unsuccessful. It moderated, however, as the afternoon wore on, and we were
again rejoiced to see the horizon broken by
the spouting *jets* of numerous whales. A
large "sconce," or rather small floe, lay some
distance a-head—round this they were playing
in dozens. All sail was crowded on at once,
though there was a strong breeze blowing,
but there being three or four other vessels
in company, it was of course necessary to
be a-head of them. This we accomplished
in gallant style ; the good old "Advice," when

well handled, clumsy as she looked, could still sail well, and, indeed, throughout the whole voyage, when we were in company with the others, I think we showed as good a pair of heels as any of them.

Well, we got into the midst of the black floundering masses; one, two, three boats were in an instant lowered, and in five minutes one of the largest of the oily giants was writhing and struggling under the tortures of a deeply planted harpoon,—"she" made rather a long and hard fight, but was ultimately subdued.

In the mean time, all the other vessels had "got fast," each had secured his whale, but the rest of the fish had beat a quick retreat. Interested as I was in the success of our own boats, I still could not help enjoying the interesting scene that was going on amongst those of the "Truelove;"—they had got fast to a large whale, but she showed better fight than any I had as yet seen. For some considerable time she lay on the surface, never diving, raising her huge tail and rump high out of the water, and lashing it into a foam, that even at the distance I was, seemed like that at the foot of Niagara. The boats

during this time lay at a respectful distance;
but soon the immense animal getting exhausted, one after the other cautiously advancing, drove their weapons into her, and she
was soon thoroughly vanquished, when the
happy conquerors found themselves possessed
of more "blubber" than their ship could well
stow, as they had previously been very fortunate.

A joyous conquest this; they were now
"full," and there was nothing, after having
"flensed" and "made off" the produce of
the dead whale, to keep them longer from
home, and "wives and sweethearts." We,
of the other ships, had been as fortunate
perhaps, but being able to stow more cargo
than the little "Truelove," could not yet think
of returning. Some of us, perhaps, looked
with envy on our lucky consort, others began
to think of preparing letters to forward by
her, glad that the good success of a neighbour
would enable us to communicate sooner with
those at home.

For some time previous to this we had become accustomed to some material difference
between night and day. I did not mention
at the time, that I saw the first star I had

seen since the beginning of May, on the 12th
of August, whilst coming out of Lancaster
Sound, dreary and dismal, disheartened and
disappointed.

The nights after this continued gradually
drawing in, and getting darker and darker.

It had now become necessary to make the
ship fast to a floe as the night fell. But
really some of those nights were beautiful
enough to compensate for any hardship or
any want. Can you conceive a sky and an
atmosphere clear and brilliant; a moon still
brighter and still more brilliant, and silvery
masses of ice lying sparkling beneath. Although it was now becoming exceedingly
cold and chilly, it was almost impossible to
tear oneself from the deck at these times.
How often I longed to be able to accurately
transfer to paper the bright tints of those
Arctic evenings, you may well conceive. I
do not think there is any region in the world
where the landscape painter could enjoy better
studies than in the Arctic regions. The sun-
sets I cannot and will not attempt to describe.
Imagine the most brilliant colours,—colours
which, in a painting, would be pronounced as
unnatural as seemingly wonderful, but which

are here beheld in all the dazzling splendour
of Nature's own design.

Our "fish" was now killed. The master,
in the "crow's nest," had his eyes by this time
on something else, being now sure of the one
the men had been for some time engaged
with. He had marked a huge black mass
some five miles a-head of us; it was a "dead
fish," worth 500*l*. at least; but stop—there
were two ships between us and the desired
prize. An old and experienced harpooner,
the only one now on board, was called into
consultation, but he could not see it; so to
make sure, with his usual energy and quick-
ness of determination, off starts the master
himself, with a well-manned boat, going cautiously at first, and slowly passing the other
ships' boats, but afterwards pushing rapidly
forward towards the desired prize. I ran up
to the crow's nest when the master left the
ship, and of course, with true *esprit de corps*,
I by all means wished to see him get the
"fish." Anxiously, then, passed the moments
until I saw him past the boats of the other
ships. I could make out the "dead fish"
distinctly; over it was hovering a large burgomaster (*Larus glaucus*), which, with the pecu-

liarity of the *Laridæ*, seldom or ever alights
on the object on which it is feeding. Luckily,
during this time, the masters of the other
ships had not been in their "crow's nest,"
being busily engaged with their captured fish,
so that they had not noticed our cautious
manœuvring. But now, one of them ascend-
ing, noticed (as he afterwards informed us)
my long form standing erect on the seat of
the "nest," with telescope fixed to my eye,
and seemingly greatly interested in what was
going on a-head of his own boats. They are
quick witted as well as quick sighted, most of
these same whaling masters, so, seeing at once
that something was in the wind, his own glass
was immediately applied in the same direction,
when he at once saw one of our pretty white
boats pulling rapidly towards an object that he
almost at the same time discerned; an object,
too, worth some little trouble to attain possession
of, but he at once saw it was too late. Had
any of the other ships seen it about the same
time we did, there would have been a hard
struggle for it, and many an arm would have
ached in the race that would have ensued.
However, our good outlook gained us possession of the valuable prize, for now I could see

those in the boat waving aloft in triumph the
blue jack. I shouted out "a fall!" to those
on deck, which was loudly and gladly responded to, and the ship's jack was again
hoisted to the mizen-top, not a little to the
astonishment, and, I dare say, causing not a
little envy amongst those of the other ships, who
had not noticed what was going on in the
"Advice." This was the third time during the
voyage that we had got "two fish at a fall."
All the boats now started rapidly off to assist in
towing our prize to the ship, which was lying
made fast to the floe. Not a soul was now
left on board but myself, the first mate, and
steward, so that for an hour or two we had a
quiet enough ship. As good honest James
(the mate) and I sat before the blazing cabin
stove, enjoying our comfortable tea, and doing
not a little damage to the cold junk and hard
biscuits, not a sound broke the stillness around
but the gentle washing of the water under the
hollow ledges of the floe, beside which we lay.
In a short time we heard the sound of oars,
and going on deck, found the master alongside,
in great spirits at the day's work. Having
something to communicate to Mr. Parker of
the "Truelove," he ordered James to take the

boat and proceed there. Always fond of the
boating, I proposed to accompany them; so,
jumping in and taking the steer oar, off we
started. The "Truelove" lay about seven
miles off. It was getting late in the evening,
but a bright moon was just rising, and we
had scarcely started from the ship, when the
loud screaming of two birds, fluttering over
head, attracted my attention. It was a
poor kittiwake (*Larus rissa*), vainly endea-
vouring to escape from its enemy the "boatswain" (*Stercorarius parasitica*). We had a
pleasant pull towards the "Truelove," the
various hummocks and masses of ice we
passed, lying sparkling beneath the moonshine,
whilst they were shadowed beyond in the
deepest blackness. I mentally repeated Sir
Walter's loved lines, and, in imagination, was
again at home amongst those who I knew
would be looking anxiously for my return.
But, alas! what had I to say; I had returned
without any news of those whose fate must
be for another year left in uncertainty.

But these melancholy musings were now
broken by the mate pointing out the "Truelove," now but a short distance from us. We
were soon alongside and aboard; James and I

met with a kind welcome from Mr. Parker.
As it was now late, we lost no time in what
we had to do, and almost immediately prepared for our return. · We started, but a
change had rapidly come over the scene,
great dark masses of clouds had now obscured the moon, and a snow storm was
coming on rapidly. We had just time, before
it became utterly obscured, to take our bear-
ings for the " Advice."   In a short time the
snow was pelting against my face with needle-
like sharpness, and it was almost impossible
to see a yard a-head. As boatsteerer, I was
necessarily the only one obliged to face the
blast, the others having their backs to it.
Besides, the boatsteerer has to stand upright
on the lines, in the stern of the boat, on a
level with the gunwale, so that I was completely exposed to its fury. I was soon one
snow-enveloped mass, but I never felt it cold,
and should indeed have been perfectly comfortable, if I could have kept the snow out
of my eyes, and been able to see a-head clearly.
I think (with all modesty be it said) that I kept
my course pretty well, for only once or twice
had the mate to say, " A little more to star-
board," or, "A little more to larboard, doctor."

And I was not a little proud, and thought
that, for a landsman, I had acquitted myself
pretty well as a boatsteerer, in a dark and
snowy night, when my eyes were greeted by
a bright light straight a-head, which we found
had been hung out by the master for our guidance, as well as for the guidance of the other
boats, the crews of which were wearily, but hap-
pily, I dare say, engaged in towing the dead fish
towards the ship, with the snowy blast drifting right in their faces. They arrived at the
same time we did ; first the long line of boats
came in sight, and then sternmost, appeared
an immense bulk, more like a dismasted ship
than any of the whales I had hitherto seen.
Fast advancing putrefaction—which, from the
immense bulk and very high degree of animal
heat peculiar to the *Cetaceæ*, commences
in those animals very soon after death,—had
caused this one to swell into this great size.
Generally speaking, the whale after death
sinks to the bottom, unless its captors have
properly secured it, when decay soon commencing, the gases generated buoy the car-
case up again. Such had been the case with
this one. It had been mortally wounded by
some of the other ships, far to the northward,

and swam thus far ere it died. It had just floated to the surface when it was first seen. Had it been floating for any time, even for an hour or two, instead of there being only one burgomaster ready to prey on it, there would have been bears in dozens, burgomasters in hundreds, and fulmars in thousands, each greedily rending and tearing at the inert mass. However, a more powerful beast of prey had secured the carrion, if one may call that carrion which will produce so much *cash*. Here it was, however, safe alongside the ship, and emitting, I must tell you, anything but a pleasant perfume; it was the first time, however, that I had to find fault with the poor whales on this account. On this occasion only, had I even the slightest reason to object to their coming between "the wind and my nobility." But the strangest of it all was, that the approach of the sweet-smelling stranger was announced by the most unearthly music, though, perhaps, it would not have been thought so by a thorough-bred Highlander; it was the bagpipes to a note—to a tone. I almost thought I could recognise a long-remembered strathspey; but where could be the bagpipes? It was soon all explained, however; the thrusts of sundry lances into the swollen carcass, had made small apertures into the abdomen, from whence issued the gas confined therein, each forward tug of the boats graduating the tension of the abdominal muscles, and at the same time graduating the emission of the gas, transformed the dead whale into a strange musical instrument.

I was not long in retiring to my berth when I got on board, tired after the excitements and fatigues of the day. During the whole of the next day, all the crew were busily engaged in taking on board the produce of the two whales; they were both good ones, and had both first-rate whalebone (baleen) in their heads, that of one of them being beautifully streaked and variegated.* From the dead fish, also, I had ex-

* There are many quaint and strange passages in those parts of "Purchase's Pilgrimes" referring to the early Arctic voyages and the early whale fishers, two of which it may not be out of place to append here,—one concerning the whalebone, the other the food of the animal.

"His head is the third part of him, his mouth (O! Hellish wide!) sixteene foot in the opening; and yet out of that *Belly of Hell*, yeelding much to the ornaments of our womene's backs; the Whalebones or Finnes being no other than the rough or inner part thereof, &c.   *   *

pected to have made something out, seeing
that its unusual buoyancy raising it higher
out of the water, I thought to have been
able to examine the contents of the stomach
and intestinal canal, besides other points of
interest, but I at once found that putrefaction
had advanced too far to allow of anything
definite to be determined.

There can be no doubt, I think, that not
only the numerous genera and species of
Entomostraca and *Acalephæ*, but that every

"His food (that Nature might teach the greatest, to be
content with, and that Greatnesse may be maintained
without Rapine, as in the Elephant, the greatest of land
creatures, and sea monsters) is grasse and weeds of the sea,
and a kind of water-worm like a beetle, whereof the Finnes
of his mouth hang full, and sometimes little birds, all which
striking the water with his tayle and making an Eddie, he
gapes and receiveth into his mouth, neither is anything
else (Master Sherwin hath seen them opened, and opened
this unto me) found in their bellies."

Of the latter extract, it need only be said that, that part
of it referring to the "water-worm like a beetle," whereof the
"Finnes of his mouth hang full" is the only truthful part of
"Master Sherwin's" report to the worthy compiler of the
"Pilgrimes." But it shows, amongst much that was incor-
rect, he was observant enough to perceive that the *Acalephæ*
and the *Clios* constituted a considerable part of the whale's
food; it being most likely one of the former which was his
"water-worm like a beetle." It shows also that he had
observed the true function of the baleen, or whalebone.

other tribe of minute animal life with which
many parts of the Arctic seas teem, form
indiscriminately the food of the huge *Mystecetus*. But there is peculiar interest attached
to the *Clio Borealis* and *Helicina* as far as
regards their relation to the food of the
whale. The former (*Clio*) amongst the men
employed in the fishery generally goes by the
name of the " whale's food." And I have been
informed by one, whom I consider a good
authority, that he considers the *Helicina* to
constitute the greater bulk of the " whale's
food," as he has always noticed that where-
ever the *Mystecetus* was numerous there also
would the water be almost blackened by this
little *Pteropod*.

Nothing can be more beautiful than the
motions and appearance of the *Clio* as seen
in the water. Its red head and wings, and
opal coloured body, with its slow and graceful
motions, render it an exceedingly interesting
and pretty object in a glass vessel. I had
intended to have brought some of them home
alive, if I could have effected it; but unluckily
the glass jar I had them in, was thrown off
the stern window lockers on which it was
standing, so that I lost the whole of them.

I managed to preserve a good many specimens in spirits, however.

I never saw them to better advantage than in Pond's Bay. During the beautiful weather which we enjoyed there, nothing could be more interesting than a walk on the floe; in every crack of the ice were to be seen *Acalephæ* of the most beautiful forms and brilliant colours,—crimson, purple, and azure, whilst their long tentacles floated gracefully beneath them; and their ever-moving cilia were brightly iridescent. The less gay, but as graceful *Clio* would be seen floating amongst them, and the sombre coloured little *Limacina* moving quickly by fits and starts; but not nearly so quickly as the merry bounding hither and thither of the bright yellow little *Gammarus* (*Gammarus Arcticus*). Fancy all these in a narrow split or crack of the floe not more than a foot and a-half wide, bounded on either side by the deep blue of the submerged part of the ice, which appears as if it were suspended to the bright white of that portion which is above water.

After the produce of our two whales had been " made off," and properly stowed away, we cast off and continued our course to the southward, keeping as close in-shore as we could. Always making fast to a floe at night, and casting off again as day broke. One morning, at this time, I noticed a beautiful gyrfalcon (*Falco gyrfalco*) soaring about the ship. I immediately got my gun ready, but he seemed to be aware that he was in a dangerous neighbourhood, and kept at a safe distance, so that I had no opportunity of getting a shot at him. He remained beside us some time, but never came within shot. His plumage was almost snowy white, and his elegant soaring flight (so different from the heavy flapping of the gulls we had been so long accustomed to, or even that of the fulmars) was very beautiful.

We now ran in towards Cape Searle, and passed close under that noble headland. I should like to have landed at Dorban, as I was informed that coal of good quality is found there. All these localities are well known to the whalers, but they have never yet been thoroughly explored, particularly the Fiords, which so deeply indent and cut up the shores. We were now fairly out of the ice, and intended making for Exeter harbour; but thick weather and a strong gale of wind coming on,

a heavy sea arose, and we were kept knocking
about for four-and-twenty hours in a most
uncomfortable state. For months accustomed
to the smooth water amongst the ice, with
the exception of the storm we experienced in
Lancaster Sound, this change was anything
but agreeable. We had the misfortune, too,
to be struck aft by a heavy sea, which washed
in all the stern windows and filled the cabin
with water, giving my books a good swim and
a thorough washing, and destroying many of
them utterly.

It moderated next day, and we ran in towards Exeter harbour. This being only the
third occasion during six long months that I
had an opportunity of landing, or even getting
a close view of the shore, I was naturally impatient at the slow progress we seemed to
make towards the black precipices before us.
A heavy swell was running, with but a light
breeze; and even well on in the day the coast,
which in the morning seemed almost close at
hand, was still far off. The breeze freshened,
however, in the afternoon, and we rapidly
approached the rocks, but where the entrance
to the harbour was I could not make out.
To my eye there was no break or opening in

the high, black wall before us; but in an
instant almost it appeared opening out as if
the wand of an enchanter had rent the preci-
pice in twain. In a few minutes we were
sailing between high walls of granite into this
strange haven, the entrance to which, although
nearly a mile in breadth, seemed narrowed into
a mere canal, from the effects of the cliffs
which rose so high over head on either side;
whilst the tower-like islands on the north, split
off as it were from the main mass, looked as
if placed there to guard and command the
entrance. We slowly made our way up the
Fiord, which strongly reminded me of the
lochs of the west coast of Scotland, though
of course the scenery was infinitely wilder.
On the south side the shores were abruptly
precipitous, as were they also on the north
side, until about three miles from the entrance,
but then, they formed a beautiful slope,—now
glowing in the evening sun, in the brightest
red, brown, and yellow, with here and there
patches of green, like one of our own moors.
But the delicious perfume that came off from
this shore—"the smell of land"—of the here
somewhat plentiful vegetation drying under
the autumn sun, was perfectly delightful. I

enjoyed it almost as much, I should think, as those are said to do who inhale the aromatic breezes which are wafted from the shores of Ceylon and the other spice islands.

When we got up to the anchorage, we found two vessels lying there. Many were the conjectures as to who they were, until, getting nearer, we found them to be the "Jane" of Bo'ness, and the "Dublin" of Peterhead. It was known to most of those on board that the "Dublin" had been at the seal fishery in spring, and that she must have been home since then. Here then was an opportunity of hearing intelligence, perhaps letters; at all events a few newspapers would be procurable. One or two of the latter we did get, but no letters. However, even a couple of provincial papers, barren enough of news, proved very acceptable. We cast anchor for the first time since leaving Stromness, and remained here for ten days. All the boats during this time were almost constantly away from the ship, leaving at four o'clock in the morning and never returning until six or seven at night. This is called the "rock nose" fishing; and hard work it is for the poor fellows in severe weather.

However, our men had been this year provided with an apparatus which greatly con-
duced to their comfort, in the shape of " conjurors " fitted up with large lamps, by which
means they could make for themselves hot
coffee or tea, as they required it, when they
were away from the ship for any time. Each
of the boats was supplied with one of these
" conjurors." The first night we lay here
the weather was most beautiful, and I could
scarcely feast my eyes sufficiently upon the
beautifully variegated shores on either side of
us.

I expected early next morning to be able
to land, and visions of ptarmigan and white
hare shooting, or perhaps a shot at a stray
rein-deer, all of which, with the exception of
the latter, were said to be very plentiful here,
filled my mind throughout the night, to say
nothing of a rich harvest of plants.

At 4 A.M. next morning all hands were
called, and I jumped up at the same time to
see that my double-barrel and rifle were in
order, but to my dismay I found on going on
deck, that it was snowing hard, and had been
doing so all night. The slopes and hills
all around us were deeply covered, and the

vivid colours of the previous evening changed
to an unbroken white. Here was a disappointment ; it continued snowing heavily
during the whole of that long day and most
of next. It was very cold, and the snow
scarcely melting when it fell in the water;
" pancake ice" began to form, and it looked
very like as if we were going to be frozen up.
However, it was too early in the season to
be at all apprehensive of that. On a former
year a Peterhead ship happened to be frozen
up in this harbour. A party of her crew
volunteered to remain with her during the
winter the rest going home in the other
ships, which, lying further out, had not been
" caught." There would have been no risk in
their doing this ; they had abundance of provisions and stores of every kind, and were,
besides, lying in a snug landlocked harbour;
but their comrades had not left them twenty
minutes when their courage failed them, and
they were seen quickly making their way after
them towards the boats which were to con-
vey them to the ships. Next season the
vessel was found lying in the same position
perfectly safe, the very remains of their last
meal being still on the cabin-table untouched

and almost unchanged. There were five ships here at the same time with ourselves, all anchored within a few yards of one another, so that the lonely Fiord of the Coast of Labrador had almost the appearance of a well-frequented roadstead. In the mornings, too (at 4 A.M.), when all hands were called, and the boats dispatched, after the men had had their breakfasts, the scene was an animated one. Six or seven boats started from each vessel. The first thing they did on starting was to fire off their harpoon guns in order to be certain that the damp had not affected the charges, so that in the early mornings we had regular salutes, which awoke the echoes from the hills and valleys around us very beautifully and distinctly; and then the boats, some thirty in number, each with their little white sails, set knowingly and daintily, would race their way down the Fiord, between its steep black sides, except when, ever and anon, a gust from some of the deep gullies on either side would make them bend and bow before it; then becoming lesser and lesser, until, in the deep blue of these clear Arctic autumn early mornings, they appeared in the distance as they emerged through the

entrance of the Fiord like a group of the tiny
nautilus. Well pleased were the men in the
evenings if they had a breeze sufficient to
bring them back, but generally speaking their
weary arms had to supply the motive power.
But happy enough they seemed to be when
they got on board; the boats were cheerily
hoisted up; then each and all betook themselves to the infusions and decoctions of their
tea and coffee, the whaling sailor's greatest
luxury and comfort. He has no objection to
his grog, but I think he has, long ere this,
found out that *hot, strong tea or coffee*, particularly the former, is by far the best beverage
he can take in these climates.

A few hands had been kept on board one
day, to bring off water with the stern boat.
Opposite the anchorage, on the south side,
were one or two deep gullies, down which
ran little streams.

I went on shore with the boat on one of
its trips. I leaped on shore as we touched the
steep beach, but not without wet feet, as even
here there was not a little surf running. I
had twice before landed on the shores of
Baffin's Bay and its inlets; at Liefly in Disco
Island, as you will remember, and at Navy

Board Inlet; but this was the first time I
had seen any thing like a beach. All that I
had hitherto seen were bluff rocks, rising
abruptly from the sea; this beach was composed of rounded pebbles of gneis and granite,
the only formations I could notice in any part
of the Fiord I saw. I wandered up the gully
a short way, my onward progress being rather
difficult over the large rounded bullets with
which it was paved, and the meandering of
the stream, from side to side, rendering it
frequently necessary to ford it at the expense
of wet feet. I found but few plants, and did
not see a single animated object with the
exception of a small bird which was briskly
hopping and chirping amongst the rocks. I
could scarcely make it out, but rather think
it was the shore lark (*Alauda cornuta*). On
my return I was tempted up a ledge on the
left side of the gully, which led me to a
soft mossy terrace overhanging the watering-
place. I saw the boat had completed her
watering, and prepared to make my way
quickly towards her. But on glancing round,
I noticed an oblong enclosure of stones, which
at first I took to be the remains of an Esquimaux encampment, but on examination I

found it to be the grave of a poor sailor, who had died of an accidental gun-shot wound, when his ship was lying in this harbour many years ago. A board, on which his name and the particulars of his death were painted, looked as fresh as if done yesterday, but no sorrowing eye of relative had ever gazed on it. The very vessel in which he had died was lying in the harbour within a few yards of his lonely and forgotten grave; manned by his townsmen and old messmates. But it would have been unvisited had not my random steps led me to it. Desolate as the spot was, it struck me that I should much rather choose such a place of sepulture than be laid in one of those disgusting charnel-yards which still disgrace our greatest cities, and in which the dismal grave stones are seen planted so thickly that there is scarce moving room amongst them.

The boats had all left the ship early one morning, when taking the " dingo " or " dingy" (I scarcely know which is the correct orthography of this kind of naval architecture, but I would advise no one to trust himself in it, under whatever name by which it may be designated), and getting one of the boys

to accompany me, and row the said "dingy,"
we set off towards the north shore of the
Fiord, trusting to find sport of some kind,
at least to have a stretching and uninterrupted
walk on the shores before us. I took with
me my double-barrelled gun, and the boy,
Jack, had procured an old rusty musket. Unfortunately (as it turned out), I did not think
of it at the time, or I would have given him
my rifle to carry, as I knew he was well
acquainted with the use of fire-arms, and
indeed, an excellent shot. However, we pulled
towards the north shore, and an uncomfortable
pull it was; a long swell was running up the
Fiord, and when we got nigh the shore we
found such a surf breaking on it that it was
impossible to land. When we left the ship
we had only been able to find two oars belonging to this same wretched "dingy." In
my impatience to be off, I did not wait for
others to be hunted out. One was the "steer
oar," and, of course, nearly half as long again
as the other. So that do as we liked we
had infinite difficulty in making our little
craft steer a straight course. There was besides
no ballast in her, so that whenever I moved
my long body we were in imminent danger

of upsetting our too buoyant little boat. However, we were not to be discouraged, so pulling up the Fiord, we rounded a point which stretches out from the north shore, and found ourselves in what the whalers call the inner or upper harbour. On this point is erected a beacon or tower, as a bearing mark for the anchorage. It was built many years ago by the man who first entered this Fiord, Mr. Gray, the master of one of the Peterhead whalers, which town, I may tell you, produces the best and most enterprising men in the whale fishery. When we had rounded the point, I was rejoiced to see numerous flocks of burgomasters, ravens, and other birds hovering over another rocky point a-head. Here, now, I thought, I shall be able to get some good birds at last. Pulling cautiously onwards, we neared the rocks. I had already noticed that the birds were disturbed and alarmed before they could possibly have noticed our cautious advance. The burgomasters were flying hither and thither in a manner very different from their usual bold, steady, flight, every now and then uttering their strange cry. The huge black ravens would alight for an instant on the equally black rocks, but after an instant, again rise hurriedly in the air, with hoarse angry croakings. There is something to be seen round these rocks, I am certain, thought I; but all the birds seemed so alarmed that I began to despair of getting a shot at them at all. I had never yet got a chance of a shot at the huge burgomaster, and, of course, I was proportionably anxious to do it.

As we rounded the point of rocks the whole was explained; a not very agreeable odour first greeted our nostrils, and our ears were almost at the same time saluted by the loud and furious growlings of a couple of immense bears, now in their turn disturbed at their banquet, as they had previously disturbed the birds. They were busily employed at the " krang," or carcass of a large whale, which one of the ships had killed a few days before, and which had been floated up here by the tide. One of them rushed furiously at us.

" I have been wishing all the voyage to get a shot at a bear, and here I am now, Jack, with two before me, and not a single ball to greet them with. And in this horrid cockle-shell of a boat too, that I can't move in. What 's the use of small shot against their shaggy hides. Not a single lance with us either. What shall we do?"

"Keep at a safe distance, sir, I advise you," said Jack, whose four years' experience in the country gave him a right to speak; "this dingy won't like the touch of a bear's paw; and besides, what can we do without lances?"

So we sheered cautiously and reluctantly off, one of the bears following, and showing his ivory tusks as he growled savagely at us. We pulled over to the other side of the Fiord, and then down towards the ship, during which time we killed a few dovekies (*Colymbus grylle*), and had besides a shot at a saddleback seal (Atack—*Phoca Grœnlandica*). I had killed it, but it sank before we got hold of it. There is nothing more annoying than this. I had often before shot these seals, and the crested or bladder nose (*Cystophora cristata*), on the east side; but if they happened to be killed outright, they invariably sank. The seals were numerous here, every now and then their strange-looking heads emerging from the water and gazing earnestly around, with curiosity absolutely depicted in their countenances. I lost many a shot at them, however, being too much taken up with the magnificence of the

cliffs under which we were passing, the summits of which seemed almost to be lost in the
clouds above.

I am certain there must be fish of many
kinds in all these Fiords. The whalers say
not:—but why are the seals so numerous?
Had I only had a seine net, I could have satisfied myself. I put overboard lines, but did
not succeed in getting fish of any kind.

As we neared the ship, I saw a bird, which
I had once seen before, but I could not manage
to get within shot of it, it was so wild and
restless. I should have taken it for the snipe,
but it seemed somewhat larger, and besides
took the water. Speaking of it to one of the
mates, he told me he knew the bird, and had
shot them often, and that their toes were half-
webbed; so I take it for granted that it must
be the *Catoptrophorus semipalmatus*.

We reached the ship, and on my telling the
Captain of the bears we had seen, he, who is
a keen bear-hunter, and has killed not a few
with his own hand, immediately made arrange-
ments to start after them. I had to endure
some bantering about not having faced them
boldly, but I do think that there was little to
be ashamed of, in declining an encounter with

H

a couple of bears as large as bullocks, with
nothing whatever in my hands but a fowling-
piece loaded with No. 4, and that in a cockle-
shell of a boat, without a single lance, should
we have come to close quarters. However,
off we set for another encounter with the
monarch of the Arctic wastes. But, better
equipped this time, in a good whale-boat,
loaded rifles and muskets, plenty of lances,
and a strong crew. Swiftly we made our way
up the Fiord, urging forwards by willing hands,
all more anxious than the other to see the
anticipated spot. We soon passed the first
point of the inner harbour, and landed between
it and the second, intending to creep quietly
over towards the " krang," and have a snug
shot at Master Bruin. Quietly we did so, but
I had already noticed a difference in the conduct of the birds; they were startled, but it
was our advance that did so; their attention
was not divided between two intruders as before—the ravens were bolder, and the burgomasters a little less shy. However, we advanced over the crest of the bluffs with rifles
ready cocked, expecting every instant to hear
the angry growl of the bears. But we walked
right up to the krang without seeing anything

of them. They had beat a retreat, and the
only trace we could find of them was a lair
in the snow where they had been sleeping,
which was deeply hollowed out into what Master Bruin, I dare say, considered a very comfortable berth. After this disappointment we
advanced a considerable way from the shore,
over a strange level tract of angular blocks of
granite, as desolate a scene as can well be conceived. Whilst cautiously stepping from block
to block, my ear was attracted by a sound
which I thought I had heard before. It was
like a short, sharp, toll of a bell, repeated at
intervals; or, perhaps, rather like a smart
blow struck upon a metallic plate. I looked
around me in astonishment, but when I saw
one or two ravens seated on the crags to the
left, and keeping a steadfast eye on our
motions, I immediately became aware of the
origin of the sound. I am not aware that
this peculiarity of the voice of the raven has
ever been noticed before; it certainly seems
somewhat paradoxical to speak of a *musical
croak*, but to my ears, at least, amongst these
wild scenes, it sounded both *musical and bell-
like*.

We now came to a small lake on which

were numerous water-fowl, but they were so wild that we did not succeed in getting within shot, even with the greatest precautions. I could not make out what they were, as even when we were at a considerable distance, they rose in a body and proceeded inland. On examination I found that this lake had been a creek or inlet of the Fiord, and that it was now only separated from it by a raised beach of small granite boulders, which stretched across the mouth of the inlet in the most regular form. The level of the water in the lagoon was evidently lower than that in the Fiord.

We returned to the ship not a little disappointed that our excursion had been a bootless one, and that we had not even a single bear-skin to show as trophy.

I had another land expedition a few days afterwards, on a Sunday, when all hands were on board. The mate and I landed on the south shore, and each armed with a lance (in case we should meet with bears, but more as a pole to assist us over our rough and rocky path), proceeded to make our way in a south-easterly direction, over the hills to the sea. We had first to climb up the steep

side of the slope before us, where every step
required to be cautiously picked, as many
of the ponderous masses of granite were so
delicately poised that the slightest touch sent
them thundering down below. We reached
the summit of the first eminence, and turned
to look upon the ships, they looked like mere
cockle-shells beneath us. For nearly ten miles
we scrambled over hills and down ravines,
forded streams, and crossed deep and rugged
gullies. It was throughout a desolate and
dreary scene, and wherever there was the
smallest spot on which vegetation could proceed the snow lay deep. There was nothing
whatever on which the eye could rest but the
rugged granite. We gained the top of the
most seaward range of mountains, and saw
that the straits before us, as far as the eye
could reach, were quite free of ice, with the
exception of a few large bergs. The prospect
all around, however, was very magnificent,
particularly inland. Our march back again
was a fatiguing one, but we reached the ship
wonderfully fresh, considering the nature of
our journey.

A few days afterwards, as not a single
whale had been seen by any of the ship's

boats, the master determined to proceed to
the southward to the gulf of Tenudiakbeek,
or Hogarth's Sound, generally called by the
whalers Kimiksoke, which is the name of
the anchoring place, a small island near the
mouth of the inlet.

We left Exeter harbour, and slowly worked
our way southward with light and baffling
breezes. In the afternoon we spoke the American ship "Mc Lellan," who was also bound
for Kimiksoke. We were now out from
under the lofty shores, and could see Mount
Raleigh's topmost peak look out from amongst
the clouds where even his lower neighbours, as
old Purchase sayeth, were "towering themselves in a lofty height, to see if they can find
refuge from those snows and colds that con-
tinualle beat them."

Next day we were off the entrance to Kimiksoke, but found that hundreds of large icebergs were scattered in every direction. The
weather looked very threatening, so the master
at once made up his mind to "bear up" for
home, much to the satisfaction of almost every
one on board; though I should have liked
exceedingly to have visited this place, about
which I had heard so much.

All hands were immediately set to work to secure the boats, &c., for the voyage, and hard work it was for them, as the storm continued gradually increasing, and the ship was scarcely made snug when it was blowing a perfect hurricane, with a tremendous sea.

Our homeward passage was exceedingly tedious; we had either calms or contrary winds, varied with heavy gales. It was nearly five weeks ere we made Cape Wrath light, and that almost at the very time we expected, so accurately had our reckoning been kept. We were becalmed off Loch Eriboll, the wild coast in which neighbourhood put us in mind of those shores we had been sailing along during the past summer. The wind sprung up during the night, however, and we had a rapid run through the Pentland Frith, landed our Orkney men at Sinclair's Bay, when the pilots came off to us, and the answer to my first question—" Has anything been heard of Sir John Franklin? " was, —" Oh! yes, sir, he 's all safe." It may be believed I leapt with joy, but was as instantly depressed, when the man continued his information, and I found it was merely that rascally Esquimaux report.

I landed at Aberdeen, and proceeded southward by mail, having been exactly eight months
on the voyage.

> Calm through the heavenly seas on high
> Comes out each white and quiet star;
> So calm up ocean's floating sky,
> Come, one by one, afar.

White quiet sails from the grim icy coasts
That hear the battles of the whaling hosts,
Whose homeward crews with feet and flutes in tune,
And spirits roughly blythe, make music to the moon.

B. SIMMONS.

THE END.

LONDON:
Printed by S. & J. BENTLEY and HENRY FLEY,
Bangor House, Shoe Lane.

For EU product safety concerns, contact us at Calle de José Abascal, 56–1°,
28003 Madrid, Spain or eugpsr@cambridge.org.

www.ingramcontent.com/pod-product-compliance
Ingram Content Group UK Ltd.
Pitfield, Milton Keynes, MK11 3LW, UK
UKHW012340130625
459647UK00009B/433